The ABC
LONDON
No. I—I
(

By

LONDON :

Ian Allan Ltd

1948

FOREWORD
to
SECOND EDITION

This new edition of the " Buses and Coaches " section of the *ABC of London's Transport* is a reprint of that published earlier in the year, though a new selection of photographs is included and the stock lists now show those vehicles which are actually operating. The value of the book is thus now considerably enhanced.

Both the Author's and the Publisher's thanks are extended to all those readers of the previous edition who have written making suggestions and criticisms, many of which have been included in this book. Their thanks are also sincerely offered to the Associated Equipment Company, the Daimler Company, the Press and Publications Officer of London Transport and to a number of members of the Omnibus Society for their invaluable help.

It is important to note that admittance to London Transport garages and works, without permission, is strictly prohibited and that the L.T.E. technical staff are, generally, too busy to attend to enthusiasts' queries unless they come through official channels.

S.L.P.

THE GENESIS OF LONDON TRANSPORT

THE size and population of the Metropolis of London has always been a major problem in recent years in connection with public passenger transport facilities. The area concerned is far greater than that of any other city, and the number of public authorities contained therein prevented anyone from being responsible for more than its own area and limited outworkings, as in the case of the tramways of the London County Council and the metropolitan boroughs and county boroughs.

The term "London area" has come to mean a huge area extending far beyond the confines of either the London County Council boundary, or even greater London, and it is continuing to expand.

In the years which followed the Great War, operation was in the hands of the underground group of companies, owning bus, railway and tramway undertakings ; the road services of Thomas Tilling Ltd. and the British Automobile Traction Co. Ltd.; the tramway services of the public authorities, and the suburban train services maintained by the main line companies grouped under the Railways Act, 1921, and those of the Metropolitan Railway.

An agreement was made by the London General Omnibus Co. Ltd. in 1921 whereby certain country areas of operation were ceded to other operators, and vehicles from the ceding company's fleet were transferred to them.

Various other agreements were concluded from time to time, and the London Traffic Act of 1924, although imposing definite restrictions on expansion by existing operators, made no attempt to unify control.

The first unification measure of comparatively recent times was tabled in the House of Commons in 1928, when the Underground group of companies and the London County Council sought powers to establish a Common

Fund and Common Management of their services. The smaller operators were to be invited to participate in the scheme.

With the change of Government in 1929, a more comprehensive measure known as the London Passenger Transport Bill was placed before the House of Commons in December, 1930.

This Bill provided that all public passenger transport within a specified area should become a state created and protected monopoly, and operation within that area was to be restricted to a corporate body known as " The London Passenger Transport Board," which body was to be empowered to acquire the whole or sections of other undertakings operating within the proposed monopoly area.

Negotiations in connection with the Bill continued until the Socialist administration was replaced by the National Government in the autumn of 1931. Considerable sums of money had been expended in these negotiations and the Bill was considered of such importance that it was carried from Session to Session of Parliament until it received the Royal Assent on 13 April, 1933.

The Board consisted of a chairman and six other members, and came into being on 1 July, 1933 ; the greater proportion of its scheduled assets being transferred to its ownership on that date. The issued share capital of the Board as shown in its Annual Report for 1946 was £112,256,508, almost all of which has been issued to constituent undertakings as consideration for their transfer to the Board, and interest paid for 1946 totalled £4,672,345.

During the war, the Government assumed control of the Board's undertaking and remained in charge. In 1947, the Transport Act established a British Transport Commission which was charged with the acquisition and public control of all inland transport. In its task, the Commission was to be assisted by a number of executives. The Board's undertaking was taken over by the London Transport Executive in exchange for Treasury guaranteed stock, on 1 January, 1948, and the Board, as such, ceased to exist.

The London Transport Executive is under the chairmanship of Lord Latham, and has four other members, responsible for staff and staff welfare, engineering, civil and electrical, supplies, legal, finance, accounts and audit, operation and mechanical engineering, respectively.

Briefly, the Board was charged under section 3 of its Act to provide a proper and co-ordinated system of passenger transport within its area ; to extend and improve that system, and conduct its undertaking and fix its fares and charges in such a manner that its revenues shall be sufficient to defray all its charges.

The London Passenger Transport area encloses the Metropolis and extends for a distance of approximately 25 miles from Charing Cross, bounded by Gravesend, Sevenoaks, East Grinstead, Crawley, Horsham, Guildford, Virginia Water, Slough, High Wycombe, Tring, Dunstable, Luton, Hitchin, Baldock, Bishop's Stortford, Chipping Ongar, Brentwood and Grays, an area of 1,986 square miles, and containing (in December, 1946) a population of 9,450,000 persons.

This area was agreed after negotiations with the operators bordering it, and adjustments were made so that the boundary generally conformed to the areas of operation worked by these concerns.

The agreements debarred the Board from working more than 10 miles beyond its boundary, even by agreement. In Kent, this outworking was limited to 5 miles, with a special provision that the Board was permitted restricted working beyond the five mile limit from Tonbridge to Tunbridge Wells, but these provisions do not apply to the London Transport Executive, which, it is legally stated, is able to run services at its discretion where it pleases.

The services worked by Birch Brothers Ltd. and the City Coach Co. Ltd. are the subject of special arrangements, while " feeder " services operated by long-distance coach operators are exempt from restriction, provided that no separate fare is charged for the service.

Within the ten mile outworking limit, the Board was subject to certain restrictions, as mentioned, and services working beyond the limits were required to be sold to the appropriate main line railway company, who transferred them to its associated road undertaking, e.g. the country bus route, Croydon to Uckfield, Sussex, had its southern portion transferred to Southdown Motor Services Ltd., although no vehicles or crews changed hands in this instance.

Within its special area, the Board had a monopoly of stage and express carriage services, and no one else may work therein, except with express written consent. These " consents," effective at 30 June, 1939, provided for the working of 1,200 services by 237 operators, mainly in connection with tours and similar events.

The Board officially divided its operations into two sections, the Central Area being approximately the Metropolitan Police District, although a number of routes extend beyond this area to reach points such as Watford, St. Albans, Slough, Windsor, Egham, Walton, Esher, Leatherhead, Farningham, Rainham, Upminster, Romford, Brentwood and Epping.

From the boundary of the Metropolitan Police District to the statutory boundary, is the sphere of the Country Bus Department, administered from Bell Street, Reigate, Surrey.

Country operation as it is understood to-day was commenced by Mr. A. H. Hawkins. In 1910, a 15 minute horse bus service connected Reigate and Redhill. On 16 March, 1911, the East Surrey Traction Co. Ltd. was formed with a capital of £2,000 and Mr. Hawkins as Managing Director, commencing operations with a Leyland double decker. In 1913, the London General Omnibus Co. Ltd. extended a number of services towards the East Surrey area, but the two companies agreed not to compete, and during the war of 1914-18, the L.G.O.C. transferred rolling stock to the East Surrey fleet. In August, 1921, the East Surrey Traction Co. became operating agents for the L.G.O.C. on a number of routes radiating from Croydon and Bromley. In 1928, East Surrey gained control of Autocar Services Ltd., of Tunbridge Wells, and in the following year the L.G.O.C. secured a controlling interest in the East Surrey Traction Co. Ltd.

On 18 January, 1932, the name was changed to London General Country Services Ltd., and it took over the routes operated on behalf of the L.G.O.C. north of the Thames by the National Omnibus and Transport Co. Ltd. and other services.

In 1930, Mr. Hawkins suggested the operation of express services under the name of "Green Line," and he eventually became Managing Director of Green Line Coaches Ltd.

On 1 July, 1933, the Board absorbed London General Country Services Ltd., and Mr. Hawkins became General Manager, Country Buses and Coaches. He retired from this position in 1945.

At its inception, the Board was without a fleetname. As repainted, tramcars had no fleetname, and for a time the buses used " GENERAL," but this was dropped early in 1934, and the buses also appeared without a fleetname as repainted. Later the present " LONDON TRANSPORT " appeared on certain vehicles mainly on route 11, and was adopted throughout, except for the coaches, which continued to use " GREEN LINE."

Liveries were, for the trams, a colour very near to that of the L.C.C. dark red " Pullman " livery, for the buses, the red and broken white of the L.G.O.C. Underground cars remained red and cream.

The Underground style of bullseye motif was retained, the colour of the circle thereof varying for the different sections, thus, white for the buses, red for the trams and trolley-buses, green for the coaches and Country Bus Department, and yellow for the railways.

The details of the setting up of the Joint Committee with the Main Line Railway Companies and the New Works Programme will be found under the sections dealing with railways and trolleybuses.

The outbreak of war in 1939 quickly affected the Board.

The Government, anticipating the need for conservation of petrol and oil fuel, made a drastic cut in the Board's supplies from 23 September, 1939, and heavy restrictions had to be made at once in the number of buses worked, and the mileage operated. 839 out of a total of 5,182 Central buses were withdrawn, and mileage was reduced by about 30%. On the Country buses and coaches the necessary economy had already been effected by the withdrawal of the Green Line coach services.

On 1 September, 1939, all Green Line coaches had been withdrawn, and ambulance equipment, manufactured before the outbreak of war, installed as the coaches came off service. Within 5 hours, over 500 coaches were ready for duty as ambulances. Most of them were immediately transferred to garages in the London area and used to evacuate hospital patients.

Limited Green Line services were restored at the direction of the Government towards the end of 1939 and in the early months of 1940 to augment travelling facilities between London and those areas where the need for additional transport was acute. These services were restored by the use of some 160 coaches released by the Government and partly by the use of double deck buses of the STL type. By the autumn of 1940 the situation in the London area was such, due to the damage to the main line railway systems and the increase in travellers, that the Government authorised the reinstatement of some of the remaining Green Line services. The more heavily used routes were operated by double deck buses and all routes terminated in London. Further restrictions, however, caused the withdrawal of Green Line services on 29 September, 1942.

In connection with evacuation, in the first four days of September, 1939, 607,635 children and adults covered by the Government evacuation scheme were removed by the Board and the main line railways from Inner London to reception areas. In this evacuation, 640 special underground trains, 4,985 buses, 533 trams and 377 trolleybuses were used. It is estimated that 1¼ million persons were carried by the Board under the various schemes of evacuation throughout the war.

During the war years, the Board turned to direct production, and had to be released by the Defence Regulations from restrictions on manufacture prescribed by its Act. The biggest contribution was in aircraft manufacture, namely the building of Handley Page Halifax bomber aircraft.

The bus fleet is working under conditions of great difficulty. The Chief Mechanical Engineer (Road Transport) has stated that as many as 400 buses have been off the road in a single day recently because of the shortage of spare parts.

The oldest buses now in service are the LT class, the first of which was put to work on 6 August, 1929, and operation has to be conducted mainly with vehicles between 7 and 18 years old. It was estimated in 1947 by normal standards that no fewer than 2,500 of the bus fleet have exceeded normal life.

A system of " cannibalisation " has been adopted whereby older buses have been dismembered to provide spare parts and vehicles actually purchased for this purpose.

LT 725 and 810 have appeared with sixty-seat bodies while major repairs are now done at garages, such as whole body sides being replaced.

The war-time standard types were built to a rigid Government specification and could only be purchased against licence, which was only granted for an essential minimum. Over the war years 710 of these types entered the Board's service. The conditions of design and manufacture of these vehicles will be found under " Guy."

There has been some misunderstanding of the conditions of manufacture of these wartime buses, and much unfair criticism. The specification aimed at a means of conveying passengers from one point to another ; manufacture was from such materials as were available, cut to a minimum quantity. Every deterioration in the situation entailed further inroads into even that minimum ; for instance, the replacement of upholstered seats by slatted wooden

9

seats, but the wartime buses have proved very satisfactory in service, which says much for the soundness of the basic design.

In passing, the question of standing passengers may be mentioned. As a wartime measure, the permissible standing had been increased to twelve persons, but soon after the end of active hostilities, it was reduced to eight. The Board (in common with other operators) wished to retain this figure until new buses became available, but trade union pressure forced a reduction to five, in strictly defined periods, principally on the ground that the Board ought to operate more vehicles. Whence they were to come was not a problem with a simple solution, but it is true that standing passengers make the conductor's task more difficult.

A memorial service was held in October, 1946, for the fallen members of the Board's staff, when it was stated that out of a total of 22,580 who had served during the war, 3,669 were still serving : 1,262 gave their lives, of whom 810 were serving in H.M. Forces, Merchant Navy and Civil Defence, while 582 were prisoners of war. Of the civilian staff, 177 were killed on duty and 275 off duty.

BUSES AND COACHES

Buses and coaches form a very large proportion of the rolling stock, and at the end of 1946, the total fleet comprised 7,027 vehicles with a combined seating capacity of 359,464 persons operating over 2,608 route miles. The passengers carried totalled 2,503,859,851 covering 50% of the Board's passenger mileage. The bus has very consistently maintained its popularity.

Central Area buses work over 1,360 miles of route, with an average of 437 buses a day per mile of road.

The Country buses operate 157 routes, totalling 1,316 miles, in an area of 1,293 square miles, or two-thirds of the Board's area, containing a population of $1\frac{1}{3}$ million persons.

RT 182 with Park Royal Coachwork   [S. L. Poole

EVOLUTION : A modern Daimler (of the D182-281 series) passing
B43 " Ole Bill " a veteran of the 1914 war

Left : A London ST
in Glasgow.

Right :
West
Riding
Gearless
Leyland
" Titan "
on
Route 13
at London
Bridge
Station.

Left :
T Class
Green
Line coach
on hire to
American
Red Cross
as a "Club
mobile."
This one
was
named
"Arkan-
sas."

"Q" type Green Line coach with Park Royal coachwork.

Q CLASS

Right : "Q" type Central Area bus with Park Royal coachwork.

Below : "Q" type on Country Service. Body by Birmingham.

[S. A. Newman

HELPING OUT : An A.E.C. "Regal" of Lily Coaches, working on route 34 is one of the 350 private-owner coaches now on hire to L.T.E.

TD 7 : A Leyland "Tiger" PS1 with MCW coachwork

[S. L. Poole

Country operations are most diverse in character, ranging from town routes in Watford, with a peak hour headway of 2½ minutes, to Dagnall Village with a bus service on Wednesdays, Saturdays and Sundays.

There are 27 Green Line coach routes on which are operated 333 coaches over 643 miles of road.

During the recent war 166 buses and coaches were totally destroyed and 4,456 damaged by enemy action.

The present-day fleet has grown out of the nucleus formed by the combined rolling stock of the London General Omnibus Co. Ltd. and London General Country Services Ltd., the former of which commenced operations in 1885, but contributions were made by Birch Brothers Ltd., originating in 1832, among others.

The term " independent proprietor," to whom the designation of " pirate " is still often loosely applied, means an operator independent of control by, or association with, the Underground group, Tilling or British Electric Traction groups, or the Main Line railway companies.

Thomas Tilling Ltd., the founder of which began as a jobmaster in 1847, were not independent proprietors in this sense, as agreements had been concluded by them with the L.G.O.C. from very early days until the final one in 1929, and working arrangements were always very close.

The part played by buses during the recent war cannot be overstated. Self-contained as regards motive power, the versatile bus was called on for duty at all hours and places. At all times, the Board held in readiness a fleet of 600 buses, with reserves, to maintain emergency services in the event of road or rail interruption by enemy action. The maximum number of buses operated on emergency services in a single day was 687.

The coming of the provincial buses to London in the autumn of 1940 will be remembered. Enemy action and other factors compelled the Board to appeal for outside help, and this came in the shape of 472 buses, lent between October, 1940, and February, 1941, by 51 provincial operators. These buses were of such diverse makes, types and ages that maintenance was extremely difficult.

The buses were a strange sight in London, with their varied liveries and makes of chassis. The memory has almost faded now, and it is hoped that the picture on page 12 will serve as a memento of days unequalled in London's history. Many of these provincial vehicles stayed but a short while in the metropolis before they had to leave to assist other cities which had suffered in air raids. The last left London by June, 1941, and many can still be seen in the provinces bearing a plate reading " LONDON 1940-41 " on the front bulkhead.

Later, the Board lent 334 buses to provincial operators on various occasions.

A new bauxite red livery with yellow reliefs appeared during the war, and at the end of 1945 the Board stated that their colour scheme was to be red (considered the most durable colour) with yellow reliefs, in which colour all the more modern vehicles were painted.

Although very common in the provinces, the wartime grey livery was seen very little in London. Guy buses G 119 to 136 inclusive and three Daimlers were delivered painted grey, and the entire complement of buses from Addlestone garage (WY) and most of Kingston's (K) single deckers were painted grey as a compulsory safety measure for working to Vickers' works at Weybridge.

The position of the Green Line coach services, which play quite a large part in London's transport facilities, may be explained here.

This service operates on what is known as " limited stop," or less commonly " express bus " working, i.e. within the Metropolitan Police District it is permitted to pick up and set down passengers only at points specified in a public time-table, and a fixed minimum fare is charged, partly to protect ordinary buses plying along the same routes, and partly to restrict the Green Line services to their proper passengers, long distance travellers.

Following the Amulree Report, a complete re-routing of all Green Line services was undertaken and new routes, avoiding the use of a Central London terminus, were instituted, such as Hertford-Guildford. A uniform scale of fares was fixed for all routes.

Upon reinstatement in 1946, all services were numbered in the " 700 " series, and later in the year, new route blinds appeared coloured yellow.

In the descriptions and stock lists which follow, the vehicles of each chassis manufacturer are grouped together in alphabetical order, beginning with the Associated Equipment Co. Ltd., and the vehicles are arranged in chronological order within the groups. This review is restricted to the present-day fleet.

In the matter of vehicle identification, bodywork often causes confusion. It was (until 1937) the practice at Chiswick, when building bodies, to provide a 3% float, that is, for every 100 chassis 103 bodies were built. Quite often, when the bus went in for overhaul, the chassis emerged with a different body, but the " float " has now been dispensed with.

" Lowbridge " bodies are referred to in the text. This is a type of body permitting the use of double deckers under most low bridges, and other places of restricted headroom. The lower overall height is obtained generally by placing the upper deck gangway at the offside, thus giving access to the seats in rows, seating alternately three and four (in some bodies, the rows all seat four), with sufficient head-room when the passenger is seated. To give sufficient headroom for the passenger to reach his seat, the gangway is dropped in the form of a long well which projects into the lower saloon above the offside seats. The type is widely used in the provinces, but very little in London.

" Unfrozen " chassis are referred to. These are chassis completed up to a certain stage, but on which the course of the war caused further work to be suspended. Later, those completed so far as to require no major manufacture of new parts, were authorised to be finished. In many cases, the manufacturer's stock of spare parts was used to complete them.

Where the term " oil engine " is used, an engine using heavy oil fuel and operating on the compression ignition system (as opposed to electric spark ignition of petrol vapour) is meant. On one downward movement of the piston, air is admitted to the cylinder and compressed on the upward movement until it is very hot ; a minute amount of oil is then injected, and a burning, rather than explosion, takes place. Oil engines are very economical in operation, and are practically fireproof, but have to be more substantially built than petrol engines, and they are heavier.

Engines of the type used in Great Britain are of the manufacturers' own patented designs, so far removed from the original designs of Dr. Diesel that it is more accurate to say " diesel type."

Stock numbers for London buses were originally metal letters and figures on a plate on the nearside of the bonnet, with transfer letters and numerals on the offside driver's cab side. The bonnet numbering was later modified to transfer letters and numerals on a plain plate, and to transfer letters and numerals direct on the bonnet side. The plates are again fitted to the post-war RTs.

Finally, the stock number appears on the inside of the rear wall of the entrance platform, together with the date of the last overhaul, or entry into service.

Vehicles common to both bus and coach use are usually distinguished by a small letter " B " or " C " after the stock number.

In the spring of 1946, the Board adopted the policy of working single deck vehicles on close headway Central Area routes to clear queues during the peak periods, for which purpose a variety of vehicles are used, labelled " RELIEF," and on 27 October, 1947, the first of some 350 coaches hired from London coach operators were put to work as relief vehicles also.

This exhausted the last reserves of vehicles, but traffic continues to increase. The Public Relations Officer stated in January, 1947, that Londoners were travelling more than ever before. In the last pre-war year, the average Londoner made 394 journeys by the Board's services, to-day's figure is well over 450. The passenger journeys originating on the whole of the Board's system in 1946 totalled 4,259,406,168 compared with the 1938-39 record of 3,782,098,000. The greatest number of passengers carried by road and rail services on one day was 15,000,000 on 28 September, 1946, a fine Saturday.

During the war, buses which came to London were allocated by official licence, but now that this system has ceased, London must take its turn on the manufacturers' waiting list for deliveries. There were 746 new buses on order for delivery during 1946, but only 225 were received. This was in addition to 69 buses with wartime standard bodies, delivered during 1946, but actually expected for 1945.

Of the 521 buses outstanding, 21 were received early in 1947. The remaining 500 were of the RT type and negotiations were concluded to purchase 1,870 more of these. Post-war orders placed for buses now total 4,000, of which 2,800 are scheduled for delivery in 1948 and 1949, but this is not certain.

The first two post-war RTs entered service in the spring of 1947, followed since by over 400 more ; but when the remainder and the first 500 Leylands are in service they will do little more than make good a part of the depreciation of the existing fleet.

Chiswick Works, the central bus and coach maintenance establishment, may be mentioned here. Opened in 1921 by the L.G.O.C., Chiswick Works have expanded considerably, and at the outbreak of war, were complete in every respect for the task of maintenance of the fleet.

A large proportion of the standard production bodies, and all the miscellaneous and experimental vehicles were built at Chiswick up to the outbreak of the recent war, while the facilities for training crews are well known.

In view of the necessity of renewing the bus fleet on a large scale in the immediate future, arrangements are being made completely to reorganise Chiswick Works so as to enable all the latest developments in factory technique to be applied to the work in hand.

Two further points relative to bodywork need explanation at this point, the first being in connection with what is referred to hereafter as the " wartime standard body," also termed " utility " and " austerity " coachwork. The body concerned was standard only in that the specification was laid down by the Ministry of Supply as the general design of a 56-seat double-deck body, with which all bodies constructed during the emergency had to comply.

All non-ferrous metals and items causing unjustified expenditure of labour were eliminated. The number of opening windows was reduced to two per deck, with the addition of long, oblong opening ventilators over the front windows upstairs and the front bulkhead window to the lower saloon. All bright plated parts disappeared and the seating was sprung upholstery, declining later to wooden slat seating.

Each coachbuilder, while keeping to the general specification, built bodies to an entirely different design, without any standardisation among the firms themselves, who were again restricted by lack of labour and material throughout.

As the war in Europe drew to its close, certain restrictions were eased and the so-called standard design improved. Aluminium was released for roof construction, tubular metal framed seating with moquette covered upholstery, plated parts, re-appeared and the number of opening windows increased.

This body is fitted to the later series of Bristols, Daimlers and Guys.

The firm called Metropolitan-Cammell-Weymann Motor Bodies Ltd. (or " MCW " for short) is a selling organisation controlled jointly by two firms of body builders, Metropolitan-Cammell Carriage and Wagon Co. Ltd. and Weymann's Ltd. Both these companies have built bus bodies for London Transport.

Experiments have been conducted with " pay-as-you-board " collection of fares on three motorbuses and two trolleybuses, but after exhaustive tests the Board stated in its Annual Report for 1946 that although " pay-as-you-board " had not proved successful, attention was still being given to finding a better system for the collection of fares than that at present in use.

BUS CLASSES

AEC

Chassis manufactured by the Associated Equipment Co. Ltd., Southall, Middlesex.

This manufacturer is responsible for by far the greater part of the chassis for the bus and coach fleet, and their *Builders of London's Buses* advertisement is as familiar a sight as the chassis itself.

The company has specialised in the production solely of passenger and commercial vehicles and power units for marine, industrial and railcar work. Its experience dates back to 1906, when the London Motor Omnibus Co. Ltd. (known as the " Vanguard ") decided to build its own chassis, and work commenced in a small shed at Walthamstow in October of that year. A subsidiary called the Motor Omnibus Construction Co. Ltd. was formed and its works began to produce in January, 1907. On 1 July, 1908, the Vanguard concern (which was the biggest motor bus proprietor in London) amalgamated with the London Road Car Co. and the L.G.O.C., and the total fleet at the end of that year numbered 962, of a variety of makes. Manufacture continued at Walthamstow, and after experiment with a number of types, the " B " type was produced and entered service on 18 October, 1910. No outside manufacturer was able to supply the L.G.O.C. requirements, and 15 of the new type were built in the first month, to go into service on route 25, then Victoria and Old Ford. In 1912, after the Underground group's acquisition of the L.G.O.C., the Walthamstow factory, expanded to 10 acres, with 1,700 employees, was transferred to the newly registered Associated Equipment Co. Ltd. Vehicle output was 30 a week. In 1926, the Associated Equipment Company moved from Walthamstow to new works at Southall, and its progress was rapid.

With the coming of the Board, the company continued as a separate entity, but the Act contained certain provisions regarding the relationship between the two undertakings. The Company supplied 90% of the Board's requirements for ten years under an agreement entered into between the two parties at the end of December, 1933. In December, 1943, this agreement was renewed for a further period of five years.

The period of service rendered by the ST and LT classes says more for the quality of the handsome vehicles produced at Southall than any advertisement. The Associated Equipment Company turned to war production, but with all the experience gained, very few minor modifications have been necessary to bring the post-war chassis into line with the most advanced present-day standards.

● ● ●

Here follow details of bus classes with chassis built by AEC and details of individual vehicles. The full lists of serial numbers are on pages 58 to 84.

¶¶LT CLASS (Total built 1429)

The oldest buses now in service. The chassis is the 6-wheel A.E.C. " Renown."

LT 1 *(54 seats)*
2 to 150 inclusive *(60 seats)*   Total 150.

LT 1 appeared on 6 August, 1929. This series has external staircases, and improved seating as compared with preceding types.

With the exceptions noted below, this particular series still retains the A.E.C. 6-cylinder petrol engine of 45 h.p. rating.

LT 21 was fitted with an oil engine some years before the recent war, but retained its external staircase body for a time, until it was replaced by an enclosed staircase body.

LT 26 also has an enclosed staircase body fitted, but retains its petrol engine.

The first 50 LTs had a square cab side and driver's dash, and although, owing to the changing around of the bodies, these appear indiscriminately throughout the external staircase series, the 50 still exist. The remainder have the rounded dash and cab side of the L.G.O.C.

LT 151 to 740 inclusive
 742 to 949 inclusive.   Total *798—56 seats*

These buses represent the second LT type, with internal staircase in one straight flight and an emergency exit at the back of the upper deck.

The seating (as built) was of brown moquette with leather facings. Push button bells and half drop windows were fitted as on LT 1 to 150.

They were built with petrol engines, but by 1940 most had been fitted with oil engines.

Indicators were standardised as roller blinds, and were the subject of much criticism when the buses first entered service, because they quoted only the route number and the extreme destination. This type of indicator was improved as in the picture on page 39, although the amount of wording shewn is the reduced wartime standard. One series had the route number removed to a box in the roof, also illustrated.

LT 741 ; 950 to 999 inclusive
 1204 to 1426 inclusive   Total *274—60 seats*

An improvement on the buses last described, with increased seating capacity, they entered service in 1931. The upper deck was taken right forward over the driver's cab and a staircase in two straight flights at right angles was incorporated. Sponge rubber seating, giving a more reclining position, was used for the first time, and metal grab rails across the seat backs replaced stanchions. Attention was given to the elimination of all fumes from the body. Destination indicators were greatly improved and criticism on this score obviated.

As built, certain of this series was fitted with petrol engines but the majority have since been converted to oil engines.

LT 964, 1235 to 1238 inclusive, and 1330 to 1354 inclusive, are still fitted with petrol engines, and work from Plumstead (AM) garage. They and the Daimlers mentioned later were the first London buses in which the fluid flywheel and self-changing, pre-selective gearbox were used.

LT 725 and 810 have been fitted with 60-seat bodies.

LT 1001 to 1050 inclusive
 1052 to 1136 inclusive
 1138 to 1201 inclusive   } Total *201—35 seats*
 1427 and 1428

Single deck buses with front entrance bodies mounted on the

23

E

A.E.C. " Renown " chassis with petrol engine. Fittings were identical with those of the contemporary series of LTs.

Some have a route indicator at the rear. LT 1427 and 1428 are ex-East Surrey Traction Co. Ltd.

LT 1000 and 1051 (2 buses)
1202 and 1203 (2 buses)   Total 4—54 seats

Four experimental double deckers produced by the L.G.O.C. on the lines of the LT class, but known as the " CC " class. Bodies were as for the 56-seat LT class.

The vehicles were sold out of service in 1939.

LT 1137

An experimental front entrance double decker produced for the Green Line services. Now scrapped.

LT 1429

A single deck petrol engined coach, mounted on an A.E.C. " Renown " chassis, with Harrington coachwork. Acquired from Edward Hillmans Saloon Coaches Ltd., and used by the Board for private hire work before the LTC class entered service. The vehicle was destroyed by enemy action in 1940.

¶ST CLASS (Total 1139)

ST	1 to 106 inclusive	
	108 to 110 inclusive	
	112 to 115 inclusive	
	117 to 128 inclusive	
	130 and 131	
	133 and 134	
	137 to 139 inclusive	Ex the **L.G.O.C.** with 49-seat
	142 only	bodies, now reduced to 48.
	144 to 151 inclusive	**Total 813.**
	153 to 156 inclusive	
	158 only	
	160 and 161	
	164 to 168 inclusive	
	170 to 817 inclusive	
	822 to 823 inclusive	
	835 and 836	

The ST class was introduced by the L.G.O.C. in January, 1930, and the class has since been extended to include all buses having the A.E.C. " Regent " short wheelbase chassis.

The L.G.O.C. series had an internal staircase body and was mounted on the " Regent " 4-wheel chassis, with 6-cylinder petrol engine rated at 37.2 h.p.

The body is similar to that of the 56-seat LTs, and has a straight staircase. At first, a large mirror was affixed to the wall of the staircase well, and there was a smaller one on the front bulkhead but these were found to serve no useful purpose, so were removed and sold to the staff. The space occupied by the stairway mirror was then utilised for an advertisement.

The ST class has proved most successful in service, and during the recent war, many were lent to operators all over Great Britain. A number were converted to producer gas operation.

ST 136 and 140
141 and 157 } Total 6 buses
162 and 163

Lowbridge buses, seating 48, with upper deck seats in the centre and a gangway each side. Ex-National Omnibus and Transport Co. Ltd.

ST 107 ; 111 ; 116 ; 129 ;
132 ; 135 ; 143 ; 152 ; } Total 13 buses
159 ; 818 ; 819 ; 820 ;
821

Buses of the same pattern as the L.G.O.C. series but ex-National Omnibus and Transport Co. Ltd. They have a smaller front destination blind box, and two-window rear platform wall, as originally fitted to the L.G.O.C. series before the latter were rebuilt in 1931.

ST 169

This is a chassis at Chiswick school and has never been fitted with a body.

ST 833 and 834
1040 to 1069 inclusive } Total 32 buses

Identical with ST 107 etc., but ex-East Surrey Traction Co. Ltd.

ST 837 to 1027—Total 191 buses

Acquired from Thomas Tilling Ltd., they have the same chassis as the L.G.O.C. series. The bodies are of Tilling construction, seat 52, have external stairs, but a different arrangement of seating. There is a single seat at the front of the lower deck (to give more clearance around the clutch casing), and a longitudinal seat at the rear of the upper deck. They had board route indicators with the destination and route number on a roller blind above. They were lent extensively during the war, and still do considerable passenger service. Some of the series are in use as training vehicles and staff canteens, and in all 69 remain. ST 1026 has a body from the ST1085 series.

ST 1028 (Scrapped 1940)
    1029 (Ditto 1946)
    1030 (Ditto 1940)
    1031 (Ditto 1940)

These buses were acquired from Metropolitan area independent proprietors.

ST 1032 to 1039 inclusive } Total 23 buses
    1070 to 1084 inclusive

County Department buses with 48 seats. The front of the upper deck is flush, and is extended right out over the driver's cab. The body is identical with LT 950 except that it is one window shorter on the length.

ST 1085 to 1088 inclusive } Total 46 buses
    1091 to 1132 inclusive

These buses are as ST 1 to 106, but have a square dash and side to the driver's cab and are ex-East Surrey Traction Co., Ltd.

ST 1089 and 1090—Total 2

Acquired from the Amersham and District Motor Bus and Haulage Co. Ltd., lowbridge buses with central seats and twin gangways on the upper deck.

ST 1133 to 1138 inclusive—Total 6

Acquired from the Lewis Omnibus Co. Ltd., (a Metropolitan Railway Associate), and now fitted with standard bodies similar to the L.G.O.C. series.

ST 1139

An open staircase bus ex-East Surrey Traction Co. Ltd., which started as a demonstration vehicle and now works from Windsor garage.

¶¶T CLASS (Total 798)

This class includes all buses mounted on the 4-wheel A.E.C. "Regal" chassis. T 1 to 402 had 6-cylinder petrol engines of 37.2 h.p. T 1 to 10 were in service by the end of 1929.

T 1 to 14 inclusive
   16 to 20 inclusive
   22 to 24 inclusive
   27 to 34 inclusive
   36 and 37 } Total 46 buses
   38 (coach, scrapped
     in 1938)
   39 to 50 inclusive
   156

Single deck buses ex-L.G.O.C. Originally had rear entrances, but were rebuilt with front entrances.

T 15 ; 21 ; 25 ; ⎫
⠀⠀⠀⠀**26 ; 35** ⎬ Total 5 buses

As the last series, but had been transferred to the East Surrey Traction Co. Ltd. They still retain their rear entrances.

T   51 to 149 inclusive ⎫
⠀⠀**155 ;** ⎬ Total 150
⠀⠀**157 to 206 inclusive** ⎭

These were the 27-seater, rear entrance coaches built for the Green Line coach services, with internal fittings on the lines of the 56-seat LTs. They have been sold out of service with the exception of those detailed under " Converted ' T ' class " on this page, and those converted to service vehicles.

T 150 to 154 inclusive—Total 5

32-seat L.G.O.C. touring coaches with canvas hooded bodies. Sold out of service in 1937.

T 207 to 306 inclusive—Total 100

30-seat, front entrance coaches for the Green Line services. Sold out of service with the exception of those detailed under " Converted ' T ' class."

CONVERTED " T " CLASS

T 208 ; 212 ; 213 ; 214 ; 215 ; 216 ; ⎫
⠀⠀**223 ; 226 ; 232 ; 234 ; 236 ; 237 ;** ⎪
⠀⠀**250 ; 253 ; 255 ; 261 ; 266 ; 267 ;** ⎬ Total 31
⠀⠀**271 ; 275 ; 276 ; 280 ; 283 ; 285 ;** ⎪
⠀⠀**296 ; 298 ; 359 ; 361 ; 362 ; 364 ;** ⎪
⠀⠀**396** ⎭

To ease the shortage of serviceable single deckers, these coaches were rebodied and fitted with A.E.C. 6-cylinder oil engines.

The bodies are of all-metal construction, with front entrance and seat 32. They had been fitted to A.E.C. " Reliance " chassis and were known as the " R " class. When these latter chassis had served their useful life, they were scrapped and the bodies mounted on the " Regals."

T 346 to 357 inclusive—Total 12

Rebodied as last described, but retained their petrol engines. The bodies were mounted direct on the " Regal " chassis, instead of on to " Reliances " first. Converted to producer gas operation during the war, and now sold out of service.

T 120 ; 209 ; 219 ; 229 ; 249 ; 252 ; ⎫
⠀⠀**262 ; 264 ; 265 ; 270 ; 277 ; 290 ;** ⎬ Total 16
⠀⠀**292 ; 297 ; 301 ; 302** ⎭

Formerly Green Line coaches, which were used as staff ambulances from September, 1939, to August, 1945, and then reverted to Country bus operation, with transverse seating.

T 207 ; 211 ; 217 ; 218 ; 230 ; 231 ;
   235 ; 239 ; 240 ; 244 ; 248 ; 251 ;   ⎫
   263 ; 273 ; 274 ; 281 ; 286 ; 288 ;   ⎬   Total 22
   291 ; 293 ; 295 ; 305   ⎭

These former Green Line coaches had their seats re-arranged longitudinally to give greater standing space, and were placed in service as buses.

T 307 to 318 inclusive—Total 12

Single deck buses ex Thomas Tilling Ltd., on the standard chassis but with Tilling-built front entrance bodies. Generally resembling the L.G.O.C. buses, they can be distinguished by the curved cab side, double mouldings on the waist line, and the route indicators, which extend nearly the full width of the roof, front and rear.

T 319 to 324 inclusive ⎫
   393 to 402 inclusive ⎬   Total 16

Coaches ex-East Surrey Traction Co. Ltd., T 393 to 398, having rather square bodies and being used for touring purposes.

T 325 to 345 inclusive

These numbers were given to 21 A.E.C. " Regal " coaches, acquired from Autocar Services Ltd., on 1 July, 1933, and immediately transferred to the Maidstone and District Motor Services Ltd. Most of them are still running for the latter operator, although rebodied.

T 346 to 357 inclusive—Total 12 (sold out of service)

The following vehicles were acquired from the proprietors shown :

T 358 ...	...	Ex-Mr. C. Aston of Watford.
T 359, 361, 362, 364, 365, 366	⎫⎬	Ex-Amersham and District Motor Bus and Haulage Co. Ltd.
T 360, 363, 367, 368	⎫⎬	Ex-Lewis Omnibus Co. Ltd.
T 369 and 371	...	Ex-Watford Omnibus Co. Ltd.
T 370 ...	...	Ex-Charles Russett & Son, St. Albans.

T 372 to 390 inclusive—Total 19

Front entrance buses ex-East Surrey Traction Co. Ltd.

T 391 and 392—Total 2

Ex-Bucks Expresses (Watford) Ltd.

T 403 to 452 inclusive—Total 50

The first series of new single deckers, classified 9T9, the bodies of which were built by the Board.

The chassis is the 4-wheel A.E.C. " Regal " with A.E.C. 7.7 litre 6-cylinder A.E.C. oil engine of 40.98 h.p. (classified by the Board as 106 mm. engine, after the cylinder bore), and fitted with fluid flywheel transmission.

The bonnet side and nearside front wing are built up into a combined structure, the casing of which includes the headlamp.

The bodies have front entrances, with sliding doors, and (as built) seated 30.

T 453 to 718 inclusive—Total 266

This series, classified 10T10, have the same chassis but the A.E.C. 8.8 litre oil engine (classified by the Board as 115 mm.) of increased horse power.   The wing and bonnet side are not built up as in the previous batch but are separate.

The body was modified slightly in design, and seating capacity varies. T 453 to 602 inclusive appeared as 30-seaters ; T 603 to 718 inclusive as 34-seaters ; many returned to service after the war as such, but some are now 31 and others 32 seaters.

The whole series of 316 vehicles has been used indiscriminately as Country buses and Green Line coaches, the small suffix " B " or " C " to the stock number being the only distinguishing feature other than the fleetname and route indicators.

During the recent war, the American Red Cross converted 55 (all from the 453 to 718 series) to " Clubmobiles," that is travelling canteens, but most have now been reconverted to coaches. Twelve have been written off.

T 719 to 768 inclusive—Total 50

Post-war single deck buses with A.E.C. " Regal " chassis, oil engine, and normal clutch and gearbox transmission.

The bodies seat 35, have front entrances, and were built by MCW.

Sliding ventilators have replaced normal opening windows.

T 769 to 798 inclusive—Total 30

These buses have the " Regal " Mark III chassis, and are a single deck version of the RT, with 31-seat body by Mann Egerton.

¶¶**STL CLASS** (*highest number 2701 ; stock numbers 131 to 152 not allocated*)

STL   1 to 50 inclusive ⎫ Total 100
     153 to 202 inclusive ⎬

In 1932 the L.G.O.C. turned from the LT class to a new vehicle mounted on the A.E.C. " Regent " 4-wheel, long wheelbase chassis, with 6-cylinder petrol engine rated at 37.2 h.p. and fitted with hydraulic brakes, servo-assisted. The design was dictated by the necessity to retain the seating capacity of 60, equal to the latest LT, while keeping the unladen weight below a legislative figure to avoid higher taxation. The increased capacity of 34 on the upper deck was obtained by projecting the upper deck forward over the driver's cab and parallel to the radiator. Internal finishings were as the 60 seat LTs and the fully floating rear axle appeared for the first time.

STL 51 to 130 inclusive—Total 80

Acquired from Thomas Tilling Ltd. and were first placed in service on 29 October, 1932. The seating capacity was 56 and the front of the upper deck inclined backwards. The chassis was the same as that of the L.G.O.C. vehicles, but most of the Tilling chassis have semi-floating rear axles.

Internally they were very handsomely finished with polished hardwood fillets and tubular seating upholstered in brown moquette.

The cab side is curved and there are two mouldings on the waist line.

STL 203 to 552 inclusive $\Big\}$ Total 400
559 to 608 inclusive

The second series produced, the first 100 by the L.G.O.C., the remainder by the Board, in which the seating capacity was reduced to 56. The front of the upper deck did not project beyond the driver's windscreen, and was inclined to the rear.

Nos. 342 to 352 were fitted with oil engines when new, the remainder with petrol engines, but most of the latter have since been converted to oil. Fluid flywheel transmission was fitted to most of this series.

STL 553 to 557 inclusive—Total 5—53 *seats*

These were built as modern open top deck vehicles on A.E.C. " Regent " chassis, with petrol engines. The bodies were built by Park Royal Coachworks Ltd., for Charles H. Pickup, an independent proprietor who favoured open top deck buses. The bodies have internal staircases and roller blind indicators. With low overall height and reduced weight, they had a remarkable turn of speed.

After acquisition by the Board, top deck covers were built on, of the STL pattern, and the buses are therefore a remarkable combination of Park Royal construction below, and Chiswick above !

The driver's dash and cab side have a curve which is very characteristic of Park Royal construction, as is the valance over the entrance platform.

STL 554 was destroyed in an air raid in 1941 ; STL 553 has been rebodied with a standard STL body of the 2189 to 2525 type from the spares " float."

STL 558
This bus has been sold out of service.

STL 609 to 958 inclusive—Total 350 buses
The first series of a type designed by the Board to replace the worn-out NS class. The chassis is the A.E.C. " Regent " long wheelbase, with a 6-cylinder oil engine rated at 40.9 h.p., fluid flywheel transmission and hydraulic brakes servo-assisted.

A new design of wood framed, metal panelled body, seating 56 was fitted. Every attempt had been made to secure the greatest possible serviceability, coupled with the ability to be produced quickly in numbers. Lamp shades and holders disappeared, the bulbs being plugged direct into the ceiling cant rail covering.

Seating is wood framed with sponge rubber cushions and backs. Rubber wings were fitted to minimise damage in collisions.
The extreme destination blind is below the route blind.

STL 1060 to 1259 inclusive—200
1264 to 1463 inclusive—200 } Total 400 buses
Of the same general design as the foregoing, but with tubular metal framed seats. The destination indicator is moved to a position above the route blind.

STL 1514 to 2013 inclusive—Total 500 buses
Of this series, 100 bodies are as described for the previous series, 360 are the same, except that the route number is set in the centre of the roof, and 40 bodies are as those of the next batch.

STL 2014 to 2188—Total 175 buses
All of the same general design but with all-metal bodies by Park Royal Coachworks Ltd.

STL 2189 to 2647—Total 459 buses
As described under STL 1514.

STL 959 to 1043 inclusive—Total 85
1056 to 1059 inclusive—Total 4 } Total 89 buses
Specially designed and built for use by the Country Department. They have wood framed, metal panelled bodies built at Chiswick, with front entrance and staircase.
The destination blind is under the route blind.
Built as 48-seaters, a number have been increased to 52 by

F

fitting seats over the wheel arches, where formerly there had been a large rack for parcels and luggage.

STL 1464 to 1513 inclusive—Total 50

This series has metal framed bodies by Weymann, of the same general design as the earlier series, but seating 48.

The seating is tubular metal framed and the destination blind is set above the route blind.

" Blackwall Tunnel " Buses

Buses for use through Blackwall and Rotherhithe Tunnels always presented designers with a problem. Originally a version of the covered top NS was used, with modified seating and a heavily domed roof to the upper deck. As these became due for replacement, a modified STL type superseded them. This latter had a shaped roof to give the necessary clearance to the Tunnel sides. The staircases were more sharply curved (reducing the seating to 55). Tyres with specially reinforced walls are used to minimise the abnormal wear from continual rubbing along the kerb through the tunnel. 40 special bodies were built, but they may not all have been fitted to chassis. When new, they were numbered between 1800 and 1900.

These buses work from Athol Street (C) garage.

STL 1167

One STL type chassis was fitted with a full fronted body like a trolleybus and numbered STF 1, but this body was later rebuilt to standard design, and numbered as above, although for the first three or four years it was numbered STL 857.

STL 1260 ; 1261 ; 1262 ; and 1263—Total 4

These are on a special shortened type of chassis with engine and transmission as the STL 609 to 1515 series, and ST pattern L.G.O.C. series bodies removed from the DST class buses. (See " D " class for further details.) STL 1262 had the body ex-DST 5, but this was replaced by an ST body, and in 1947 an STL body was fitted with standard chassis side members and other items.

STL 1044 to 1055 inclusive—Total 12

These were ordered by London General Country Services Ltd., but were not delivered until the Board had taken over. They have lowbridge, front entrance bodies by Weymann on A.E.C. " Regent " oil engined chassis. The entrances are fitted with sliding doors.

The foregoing represents the STL class as at 1939, but more vehicles have been added as follows :

STL 1617 ; 1954 ; 1955 ; 1959 ; 1973 ; 1974 ;
1978 ; 1990 ; 2107 ; 2148 ; 2186 ; 2217 ; } Total 20 buses
2220 ; 2229 ; 2232 ; 2250 ; 2273 ; 2291 ;
2292 ; 2311

Lowbridge type bodies built in 1942 and 1943 mounted on chassis which had previously been equipped with standard bodies, as described for the series in which they are numbered.

STL 2648 to 2681 inclusive—Total 34 buses

34 unfrozen chassis, with normal clutch and gearbox instead of fluid flywheel transmission. They were delivered in 1941 and 1942, and in view of the delays in production of the 34 bodies which were being built at Chiswick to fit them, 18 of them had to be fitted with a variety of old bodies, some of the 60- and early 56-seat types, which had previously been part of the spare "float." A further three were fitted with new bodies of almost standard type which were being built at the time as part of twelve replacements for bodies detroyed in air raids. Only 13 of these 34 chassis therefore received the new bodies which were being built for them. The fourteenth new body in due course joined the spares "float."

The other twenty, being of the special lowbridge type, were wanted in service as soon as they were built, so they were mounted on the first 20 of the older chassis that became available, and the standard bodies from these latter joined the "float."

STL 2682 to 2701 inclusive—Total 20

A new delivery to the Country Department in 1946.

Mounted on the post-war A.E.C. "Regent" chassis, they have bodies by MCW as supplied to provincial operators and differ from the standard London Transport bodies.

¶¶Q CLASS

Readers who study the placing of the engine will have observed how little variation there has been over the years. Originally, the engine was placed forward in the chassis, with the driver seated behind, as in a motor car, and it was not until the arrival of the L.G.O.C. "K" type in 1919 that the driver's seat was moved to a position beside the engine so as to allow a longer passenger saloon. Thereafter, this arrangement, known as "forward control," became standard. As time went on, improved methods of construction, cooling, lubrication and auxiliary fittings obviated the necessity for any fixed position of engine.

Q 1, a distinct break from accepted tradition, was produced by the Associated Equipment Company in 1932. A single deck vehicle, the engine was set upright on the offside outside the chassis frame, and the drive was taken through fluid flywheel transmission to the rear axle. The 6-cylinder petrol engine had all its auxiliary fittings, such as dynamo, water pump and the like, on the offside. The radiator was in front of the power unit, behind the offside front wheel.

The front wheels were set well back from the front end of the chassis. It had originally been intended to fit an underframe lifeguard of tramcar pattern, but it was never fitted on general production vehicles.

Single rear wheels were used, not the twin wheels normally used on heavy chassis. On Q 1 a body seating 37 was mounted, and the vehicle entered service on route 11 in September, 1932.

Experiments with the Q pattern continued. Q 2 and 3 were front entrance double deckers, Q 4 and 5 were double deckers ; Q 188 was to be a prototype for a 6-wheel double deck Green Line coach, but never ran as such. Q 1 to 5 and 188 have now been sold out of service.

The Board ordered the Q design for quantity construction, and in bodies built for them a longitudinal seat on the offside covered the engine. The A.E.C. oil engine replaced the petrol power unit of the first of the class.

The sub-divisions of the present class are as follows :

Q 6 to 105 inclusive
186 and 187 } Total 102

Buses for the Country Department with central entrance bodies built by the Birmingham Railway Carriage and Wagon Co. Ltd. The body is high at the foot and slopes down to the rear.

Q 106 to 185 inclusive—Total 80

For the Central and Country Department. The bodies are by Park Royal Coachworks Ltd., and have the entrance right forward in front of the front wheels, and are without the roof slope previously mentioned. The driver is able to keep the entrance platform under observation during loading and unloading.

Q 189 to 238 inclusive—Total 50

Coaches for the Green Line services which entered service in 1936. The coachwork is by Park Royal Coachworks Ltd., and has a central sliding door. A small intake grille at the front serves the purpose of supplying air to the radiator. Heated air is used to warm the interior of the vehicle.

Headlamps are set flush with the front of the vehicle, and the casing of these lamps incorporates the side lamps. The coaches were in service as ambulances during the recent war.

¶LTC CLASS (1 to 24 inclusive)

The chassis of the LTC class is the A.E.C. 6-wheel " Renown," with petrol engine and fluid flywheel transmission.

The body, which was constructed by the Board, has a front entrance, and incorporates a sliding roof. The rear seats are raised to give wider vision.

Since the war, the LTC vehicles have reappeared as private hire coaches, and have been acting as relief vehicles on Central and Country bus routes and also Green Line coach services.

¶RT CLASS

This type was placed in service immediately prior to the outbreak of war. It represented the most modern example of a double deck vehicle, and is the future standard.

The chassis is the A.E.C. " Regent " Mark III, with A.E.C. 6-cylinder oil engine of 53.75 h.p. with an improved form of anti-vibration rubber mounting. The chassis incorporates many improvements, including compressed air operation of brakes, gears and chassis lubrication.

Fluid flywheel transmission is incorporated, and the preselective gearbox is controlled by a small lever mounted beneath the steering wheel. By intercoupling with the braking system, the gears cannot be engaged if there is insufficient air pressure to operate the brakes.

The body seats 56 and is an improvement on that of the STLs, with a more spacious platform and more room on the staircase. The driver's cab is completely enclosed and has a sliding door.

Disc covers are fitted to the rear wheels, while the radiator has been modified in shape as compared with the STL, and set lower in the chassis to improve the driver's visibility. There is no provision for a starting handle.

The chassis of RT 1 when completed was given an open staircase body to enable it to run to gain operating experience, and the vehicle was numbered ST 1140. An experimental body was produced by February, 1939, and mounted on the chassis, the vehicle then being numbered RT 1.

The production series of buses was numbered RT 2 to 151, manufacture being suspended when this number was reached. It was stated by the manufacturers in October, 1946, that each bus had then travelled 227,000 miles, making a total mileage of 34,050,000 miles for the 150 vehicles.

During air raids, the body of RT 97 was severely damaged and was rebuilt as a " pay-as-you-board " type ; it worked in the

Central Area until March, 1946, was then painted in Green Line livery and sent to Romford garage for experimental working on routes 721 and 722.

RT 19 has a special history ; it toured England and Scotland as a demonstration vehicle and was brought back into London service.

RT 4 and RT 39, together with two provincial buses which had visited the metropolis during the emergency period, took part in the mechanised column of the London Victory Parade.

The Board, in its Annual Report for 1945, stated that valuable experience had been gained with the RT type, which was to be continued.

The first two of the post-war RTs (RT 152 and RT 402) entered service in June, 1947, and the design of the post-war body has been modified, to permit interchangeability and mass production. More have since appeared. The bodies of RT 152 to 401 were built by Park Royal, RT 402 to 651 by MCW, but work is also in hand by Saunders Engineering and Shipyard Ltd., at their Beaumaris works, in Anglesey, and by other contractors. The Saunders' bodies are expected to be delivered late in 1948.

The new series was intended to cease for the Central Area at RT 651, but when the whole of the RT 152 to 401 series was in service, certain chassis which were to have received bodies and been numbered in the RT 402 to 651 series were transferred and bodied by Park Royal. These latter were numbered RT 652 onwards.

To enable actual observations to be noted, the stock list on page 80 has been extended to RT 1000 in italic type.

BRISTOL

Chassis manufactured by the
Bristol Tramways and Carriage Co. Ltd.

(Complete list of Running Numbers on page 78)

This manufacturer's products are in wide use throughout the United Kingdom, and have earned for themselves a reputation for reliability and economy in upkeep.

The Company was registered on 1 October, 1887, to amalgamate the Bristol Tramways Co. Ltd. and the Bristol Cab Co. Ltd., and is notable for being one of the few operators not only to manufacture its own chassis, but to supply them to others.

¶¶B CLASS (first series, 1 to 9 inclusive)

This type which was placed in service in June, 1942, has the Bristol K5G chassis, with 5-cylinder Gardner oil engine, rated at 36.5 h.p. The engine manufacturers claim that by careful control of the fuel injection, the power stroke of the engine can be so regulated that its turning effort is almost equal to that of a 6-cylinder unit, with the advantage that the 5-cylinder Gardner is shorter, and could be given heavier main bearings.

The wartime version of the chassis was considerably heavier than usual owing to the wartime embargo on aluminium and its alloys.

Transmission is by normal clutch and gearbox.

Bodies of the wartime standard type, as described, are built by Park Royal Coachworks Ltd.

The Bristols were sent to Hanwell (HW) garage and work route 97.

B 10 to 29 inclusive—Total 20 buses

The second series of Bristols, placed in service at the end of 1945, with the K6A (W3 series) chassis, and the A.E.C. 6-cylinder oil engine. The radiator has been modified in shape from that of the K5G and lowered to give better all-round visibility for the driver. It has a distinct taper from top to bottom.

The fuel feed is by autovac and the square tank, an unusual sight on modern chassis, is visible beside the bonnet.

The bodywork, which is by Duple Motor Bodies, Ltd., is an advance on the previous pattern, but the overall height remains at 14 ft. 6 in.

———

DAIMLER
Chassis manufactured by the Daimler Co. Ltd. of Coventry, and sold by Transport Vehicles (Daimler) Ltd.
(Full list of Running Numbers on page 76)

The Daimler Co. Ltd., which celebrated its Jubilee in 1945, has been associated with passenger vehicles since the outset of motor operation, and it has been truthfully said " There is something different about a Daimler."

A notable landmark in the Company's history was the production of the 1912 type CC 30 chassis, designed specially for service in London. 350 vehicles were supplied to the Metropolitan Electric Tramways Ltd., some of which saw service in France during the 1914-18 war.

The British Automobile Traction Co. Ltd. purchased 33 of these vehicles, the first of which entered service on 7 October, 1912, on routes 3 and 59, and later 24. It says much for these vehicles that they survived in service until 1927.

Association between Daimler and the L.G.O.C. commenced with the supply of 30 h.p. sleeve valve engines for the latter company's chassis in 1910 and in 1912 the Associated Equipment Co. Ltd. was formed jointly by Daimler and the London General Omnibus Co., to manufacture buses for the latter. Later, the Daimler Company relinquished its interest in the Associated Equipment Co. Ltd., until on 25 June, 1926, a new concern, the Associated Daimler Co. Ltd. was formed to handle the combined commercial vehicle interests of both companies and for the interchange of experience in design and research. The trademark " ADC " was used.

The LS or " London Six " class of six wheelers was produced under this arrangement and appeared on 4 June, 1927. The double deckers settled down on route 16 from Cricklewood (W) garage, and passed to the Board.

A few still remain, but these have been converted to breakdown tenders and have been rebuilt so as to be unrecognisable.

When each company recommenced production on its own account, the Daimler Company placed the CF 6 chassis on the market, followed by the CH 6. This latter was a forward control, four wheel chassis, with 6-cylinder double sleeve valve engine, and the now well-known Daimler fluid flywheel and preselective gearbox system of transmission was fitted for the first time to a bus, as standard.

This is the one form of automatic gear control which has successfully stood the test of time and operation and

LT CLASS

Above
LT 2 :
External
Staircase
(petrol
engine)

*Right and
Below :*
Oil
engined
interior
staitcase
buses

[*B. V. Franey*

LT
753

LT
1303

LT 1109 : A single-deck LT class vehicle

STD 154 : A Leyland "Titan" PD1 with Leyland body

[S. L. Poole

D CLASS

Right : D 146—
Daimler chassis with
Duple body, work-
ing Green Line
service.

G CLASS

Below : G 407 —
Latest series Guy
"Arab" with MCW
coachwork.

B CLASS

Left : B 24—Bristol
K6A chassis with
AEC oil engine and
Duple body.

Above : Ex-L.G.O.C. T type bus.

Below : T 774, the latest single decker bus. Coachwork by Mann Eggerton.

T 502c — typical Gre Line coach the 10T series. Simi vehicles a also in serv as buses countr routes.

Above : T 267, a " converted T "
type vehicle.

Below : The post-war version of
the T type. Coachwork is by
MCW (T 733).

B. V. Franey

RT 441 : One of London's newest buses.

ST 959 : One of the few remaining Tilling ST type buses.

[S. L. Poole

ST 208 : A typical member of the ST class

[B. V. Franey

C 32—A 20-seat bus

C III—One of the "Inter-station C" buses, this bears the title
"Channel Island Airways."

enjoys the advantage that it works as well with an oil engine as with petrol. Results are best with an oil engine, as the cushion of oil in the flywheel helps to damp the more pronounced vibration encountered with this type of power unit.

Misunderstanding as to this form of transmission may be cleared up here. The fluid flywheel is a Vulcan-Sinclair patent, and is fitted to buses sold by Transport Vehicles (Daimler) Ltd. The preselective gearbox is manufactured under Wilson patents improved by patented Daimler modifications, which patents were subsequently acquired by the Self-Changing Gear Co. Ltd. Actually, this system was tested in a bus chassis before application to private cars.

The pre-selective gearbox must be regarded as complementary to the fluid flywheel as the latter allows sufficient power to be transmitted at the appropriate times to allow the gearbox to function under the most efficient conditions. The desired gear is preselected by a small lever mounted under the steering wheel, but is not changed until the gear changing pedal, occupying the position of the normal clutch pedal, is pressed. Then the desired gear is automatically engaged or changed without further effort on the driver's part.

The most impressive demonstration of the effectiveness of the transmission system is when, with the bus travelling forward, reverse gear is engaged ; the vehicle comes to a gentle stop and commences to run backwards. In emergency the reverse gear may be used as a powerful brake without damage to the transmission.

Licences have been granted to American manufacturers to fit the fluid flywheel.

Fluid flywheel transmission is also fitted to many chassis supplied by the Associated Equipment Company, who have manufactured the equipment under licence since 1934, the gearbox being operated by compressed air in some models (as the London RT). Control of the gearbox in A.E.C. vehicles (except the RT) is by a lever of the same size and position as in a normal gearbox.

The TF class of coaches is similarly fitted.

When the CH 6 appeared on the market, the L.G.O.C. ordered three, upon which were mounted bodies of the ST pattern. The vehicles were numbered in a new class, DST, sent to Harrow Weald (HD) garage, and put to work on route 18.

A number of 60-seat LTs were fitted with fluid flywheel transmission manufactured by the Daimler Company, and later the system was standardised by the L.G.O.C. and the Board, a bold step which has been fully justified.

The Daimlers were sold out of service at the end of 1934, the bodies being retained and used as described under STL 1260 to 1263.

With the coming of the war, the Daimler Company turned from its normal activities to aircraft and military vehicle production, but in 1942 it was able to re-organise its works to produce a wartime edition of its COG 5 chassis, the CWG 5, of which, however, none came to London. In 1944, the company produced a wartime CWA 6 with A.E.C. 6-cylinder oil engine and fluid flywheel transmission, and of this type London received an allocation. The design followed generally the lines of the pre-war chassis, and departures were due to wartime restrictions. The fluted-top radiator was retained, but is a most austere production with pressed steel shell and wire mesh front. The vehicles were placed in class " D " which is sub-divided as follows :

D   1 to   6 inclusive
128 to 131 inclusive } Total 10 buses

The first six, delivered in May, 1944, and four, delivered in November, 1945, make up a total of 10 lowbridge buses for working route 127. D 128 to 131 have moquette upholstered seats on tubular steel frames. The front of the dropped upper deck gangway projects into the driver's cab.

D 7 to 126 inclusive—Total 120 buses

These buses have 56-seat double deck bodies of the normal height, wartime construction. These buses entered service between August, 1944, and July, 1945.

D 133 to 137 inclusive
    141 only
    143 to 149 inclusive
    151 to 154 inclusive   Total 37 buses
    156 to 159 inclusive
    161 only
    164 to 170 inclusive
    172 to 179 inclusive

These are double deckers for the Green Line services, on CWA 6 chassis, but with an improved body by Duple.

Their livery is distinctive green with '' Green Line '' as a fleet name.

D 127 ; 132 ; 138 ; 139 ; 140 ; Total 14 buses with CWD 6
    142 ; 150 ; 155 ; 160 ; 162 ; chassis and Daimler 6-cylinder
    163 ; 171 ; 180 ; 181   oil engine.

When oil engines were introduced to bus work, the Daimler Company fitted a proprietary make of engine, but in 1936, development of the Company's own engine began. In the Coventry air raids of 1940, the Company's experimental shops, drawings and prototype oil engine were all destroyed. It was not until production of wartime buses started, using proprietary engines, that work was resumed in connection with the Daimler engine.

The CWD 6 chassis appeared in 1945, with Daimler 6-cylinder oil engine ; the chassis is of an entirely new design, of which practically all the components (including the rear axle) are of the Daimler Company's own manufacture, whereas, by arrangement with the Ministry of Supply, components of earlier wartime chassis had to be obtained from outside manufacturers. The new chassis was designed to stand up to a period between major overhauls of two years, or something over 100,000 miles. The oil engine is rated at 48 h.p. and the chassis is the normal four wheel pattern, with an improved fluid flywheel transmission system. The radiator is a more refined fitting with vertical slats. These 14 CWD 6 buses came to London.

The bodywork is identical, except for the painting with the 37 Green Line buses mentioned.

D 127 has a Daimler engine, but is identical with D 93 to 126, having been delivered four months before the CWD series.

Of the foregoing, the Green Line buses are at Romford (RE) garage, and the remainder at Merton (AL).

D 182 to 281 inclusive—Total 100 buses

This is the latest series, placed in service from Sutton (A) garage in 1946.

The chassis is the Daimler CWA 6 with an improved radiator (similar to that of the CWD 6) and bodies by Park Royal Coachworks Ltd., representing a transitional type between war and peacetime standards, and fitted with the Board's standard destination and route indicators.

Coachwork is by the following builders :

Duple Motor Bodies Ltd. Nos. 1-34, 74-92, 128-31, 132-181*.
Brush Coachwork Ltd. Nos. 35-73, 93-127.
Park Royal Coachworks Ltd. Nos. 182-281.

GUY
Chassis manufactured by Guy Motors Ltd., of Wolverhampton.
(Full list of Running Numbers on pages 76-77)

This manufacturer is responsible to the largest class of wartime buses in London.

The company was registered on 2 October, 1914, and is manufacturer of commercial motor vehicles for all purposes, and of trolleybuses.

Guy vehicles are by no means newcomers to the metropolis. Six-wheelers were supplied to the London Public Omnibus Co. Ltd. in 1927, others were supplied to independent proprietors and acquired by the Board, and during the dark days of 1940 five six-wheel double deck Guys were borrowed from Northampton Corporation from 26 October to 28 December.

When the trend of the war became apparent it was decided by the Government that a replacement double decker was essential, so the task of building a chassis to take a 56-seat body was entrusted to Guy Motors Ltd. The specification to which the vehicle was to be built was drawn up and agreed with the Ministry of Supply, the Ministry of War Transport and a Technical Committee of operators.

The basic design was that of the pre-war Guy " Arab " 4-wheel forward control chassis, with normal clutch and transmission and 5-cylinder Gardner oil engine, but all refinements had to be eliminated, and the use of aluminium

---

*Nos. 132-181 and 182 to 281 with improved pattern of wartime coachwork.

and elektron alloys strictly prohibited. This resulted in an increase of chassis weight of approximately 18.5% and the weight of the completed vehicle, depending on the make of the body, showed an increase of 13.9 to 19.5%.

For the more difficult provincial routes, the Gardner 6-cylinder engine was fitted, but sufficient supplies were available only for these conditions. After the first 500, however, the bonnets were lengthened to take the longer engine, but all the London series have the Gardner 5-cylinder engine, of the type mentioned in the Bristol K5G (B1 to 9).

The first of these Guy buses in London service appeared from Tottenham (AR) garage in the autumn of 1942. Bodies were of the wartime standard pattern.

Coachwork is by the following builders :

Park Royal Coachworks. No. 1-31* ; 51-136 ; 150 ; 206-218 ; 319-357 ; 431-435.

MCW. Nos. 32-42 ; 44-50 ; 137 and 138 ; 369-430.

Duple Motor Bodies Ltd. No. 43.

Northern Coachbuilders Ltd. Nos. 139-149 ; 151-153 ; 194-205.

Northern Counties Motor Body Building and Engineering Co. Ltd. Nos. 154-173 ; 219-257 ; 269-311.

Massey Brothers. Nos. 174-193 ; 258-268 ; 312-318 ; 358-368.

Of the London series, in all but the first 71, the radiator projects 5 in. in front of the driver's dash.

A new class G was formed and the buses numbered to 435 therein. They have proved economical and successful in service.

LEYLAND

Chassis manufactured by Leyland Motors, Ltd., Leyland, Lancs.

(Full list of Running Numbers on pages 81-84)

Leyland specialised in the production of commercial vehicles, and is to-day one of the leaders in this particular field.

The company originated as the Lancashire Steam Motor Company in 1896, and became a limited company in 1903.

* G 30 original body was destroyed in air raid and replaced by one specially built by Northern Coachbuilders Ltd.

Steam road wagons were built, and on 30 April, 1907, the company was renamed Leyland Motors Ltd.

The company's products were soon well known in London. In 1906 vehicles were supplied to the London Central Omnibus Co. Ltd., which in the same year ran the first bus along the then newly opened Kingsway. The first independent operator in London after the first Great War commenced business with a Leyland open top bus, while covered top Leyland " Titans " made by far the greater part of the vehicles acquired by the Board from the London independent proprietors.

In addition to the 8 ft. wide vehicles mentioned later, there are 1,000 " Titan " 7 ft. 6 in. chassis and 100 " Tiger " single decker chassis on order.

¶¶STD CLASS (1 to 176 inclusive)
The first series STD 1 to 100 inclusive

The first 100 vehicles delivered in 1937 had the " Titan " TD 4 four-wheel chassis, with 6-cylinder Leyland oil engine rates at 48.6 h.p. and normal transmission (except for the last ten).

The Leyland metal framed body, modified in minor details to comform to the contemporary STL, seated 56.

The last ten of the series had the Leyland hydraulic torque converter, which was a device containing an oil pump and turbine, and eliminated the normal clutch and gearbox. This equipment was removed in 1938 and replaced by normal clutch and gearbox.

The new class STD was then started, the vehicles being allocated to Hendon (AE) garage.

STD 101 to 111 inclusive—Total 11

These were unfrozen " Titan " TD 7 chassis delivered after the outbreak of war, but the bodies were very different from the previous type, being for the first time of the wartime standard pattern. These wartime " Titans " were sent to Victoria (GM) garage.

STD 112 to 176 inclusive—Total 65

Placed in service in the autumn of 1946. The chassis is the 4-wheel Leyland " Titan " PD 1 of post-war design, and is very considerably modified from those already mentioned, embodying all the wartime experience of the manufacturer. The power unit is the new 6-cylinder Leyland 7.4 litre oil engine, developing 100 b.h.p. as against the 94 b.h.p. of the pre-war engine. The radiator has been modified in shape and the filler cap offset to the nearside to allow the driver's cab to be set further forward.

The 56-seat body is by Leyland modified to the Board's requirements. Tubular seating is used, and the interior is finished in the Board's standard style. The bell-cord has reappeared and is fitted along the roof of the lower deck.

This series of buses is at Victoria (GM), Hanwell (HW) and Loughton (L) garages.

¶RTL CLASS (I to 50I inclusive)

These buses are to have the Leyland " Titan " PD2 chassis, 8 ft. wide, with oil engine of 130 b.h.p. and Leyland bodies. Other than for minor details, the vehicles will be identical in appearance with STD 112.

Assembly is expected to commence during the summer of 1948.

The extra width will be used to provide wider seats and gangways.

As ordered, the vehicles are to have fluid flywheel, and preselective, self-changing gearboxes.

RTL 501 is an experimental 7 ft. 6 in. wide chassis completed in 1948.

¶C CLASS (C I to 98 and I06 to II3 inclusive)

One of the greatest of the Board's difficulties at the outset was the lack of serviceable vehicles for the Country area, which was served by a variety of types, ranging from double deckers to Fords. Seven Central Area " Titans " were sent to help. The Qs and Country series of STL have already been mentioned, but there was a demand for buses of smaller capacity to work where conditions did not permit, and the traffic did not demand, a vehicle of normal size.

The " C " class was introduced in 1935 and has the Leyland " Cub " four-wheel chassis, with the driver seated behind the engine. All have the Leyland 6-cylinder oil engine rated at 27.3 h.p. The bodies are suitable for use either on the " one man " plan, where the driver collects the fares, or in the normal manner. The entrance is at the front, and the seating capacity is 20. C 1 started work on Central Area route 237 and, except for C 76, preceded the others by a considerable period.

Several units of the class have been sold.

C 106 to 113 inclusive—Total 8

The Board took over the inter-station bus working (on behalf of the main line railways) from a private contractor, and provided the special C buses for the service.

The chassis is the petrol engined, forward control Leyland " Cub," with a special body by Park Royal Coachworks Ltd., and a so-called " observation " rear portion, i.e. the rear seats are raised upon a platform, and the space underneath is used for luggage storage. A blue and cream livery has been adopted for the inter-station buses.

The services was reinstated after the war as an evening operation.

Coachwork is by the following builders :

L.P.T.B. Chiswick. No. 1.

Short Bros. Nos. 2-75.

Acquired from Chas. Russett & Son, " St. Albans and District." No. 76.

Metro-Cammell-Weymann. Nos. 77-98.

Park Royal Coachworks Ltd. Nos. 106-113 (inter-station).

———

¶¶CR CLASS (1 to 49 inclusive)

This class, which appeared in 1939, is developed from the C class. The endeavour to break away from the traditional position of engine and transmission has already been noted under Q, and the CR is a modified Leyland " Cub " with the engine at the rear, which concentrates the power near its point of application, the rear wheels.

The CR seats 20, and the engine is placed lengthwise at the rear of the vehicle. The emergency exit door is a door half way along the offside. The entrance behind the nearside front wheel has an electro-pneumatically operated sliding door.

These buses were withdrawn from service during the war and stored ; they re-appeared as relief buses in the Central Area during 1946.

———

¶¶TF CLASS (1 to 88 inclusive)

This type, like the Q, is an attempt to improve upon the traditional arrangement of power unit and transmission line. Modern engine design has done away with the necessity to have the engine upright, and in this model, evolved after much experimenting by the Board's engineers in collaboration with Leyland Motors Ltd.

the power unit, a 6-cylinder Leyland oil engine, is removed to an amidships position and placed on its side, underneath the floor.

Fluid flywheel transmission is incorporated for the first time in a Leyland chassis, and the preselective gearbox is operated by an air cylinder. The radiator is alongside the driver's cab on the nearside, and the driver enters his cab from inside the vehicle.

TF 2 to 13 were ordered as private hire with curved glass panels to the roof and an opening head, but with the exception of TF 9, all were destroyed by enemy action in 1940.

TF 1 has been sold out of service, while TF 14 to 88 inclusive are Green Line coaches, which were in service as ambulances during the war.

¶TD CLASS (1 to 31 inclusive)

This is the Board's latest type of single decker, placed in service late in 1946. The TD classification had previously been in use by the Board.

The chassis is the Leyland " Tiger " PS 1, the single deck version of the " Titan " PD 1, which it generally resembles.

The bodywork is by MCW as described for T 719.

GARAGES

Central and Country area buses and coaches operate from a large number of garages, listed below. The garage code and running number appear on a removable stencil plate, carried on the waistline on both sides of the vehicle.

Central Area

Code	Garage	Code	Garage
A	Sutton	J	Holloway
AB	Twickenham	K	Kingston
AC	Willesden	L	Loughton
AD	Palmers Green	M	Mortlake
AE	Hendon	MH	Muswell Hill
AF	Chelverton Road, Putney	N	Norwood
		ON	Alperton
AH	Nunhead	P	Old Kent Road
AK	Streatham	PB	Potters Bar
AL	Merton	Q	Camberwell
AM	Plumstead	R	Hammersmith
AP	Seven Kings	RD	Hornchurch
AR	Tottenham	S	Shepherds Bush
AV	Hounslow	SP	Sidcup
B	Battersea	T	Leyton
BK	Barking	TB	Bromley
C	Athol Street, Poplar	TC	Croydon
		TL	Catford
CF	Chalk Farm	U	Upton Park
CL	Clay Hall, Old Ford	UX	Uxbridge
		V	Turnham Green
D	Dalston	W	Cricklewood
E	Enfield	WG	West Green
ED	Elmers End	X	Middle Row, North Kensington
EW	Edgware		
F	Putney Bridge		
G	Forest Gate	CS	Chiswick (*not used for operational purposes*)
GM	Victoria		
H	Hackney		
HD	Harrow Weald		
HW	Hanwell		

Country Area Garages

Code	Garage	Code	Garage
CM	Chelsham	LH	Leatherhead
CY	Crawley	LS	Luton
DG	Dunton Green	MA	Amersham
DS	Dorking	NF	Northfleet
DT	Dartford	RE	Romford
EG	East Grinstead	RG	Reigate
EP	Epping	SA	St. Albans
GD	Godstone	SJ	Swanley
GF	Guildford	ST	Staines
GY	Grays	TG	Tring
HE	High Wycombe	TW	Tunbridge Wells (*)
HF	Hatfield	WA	Watford (High St.)
HG	Hertford	WR	Windsor
HH	Hemel Hempstead	WT	Watford (Leavesden
HN	Hitchin	WY	Addlestone [Rd.)

* During the latter part of the war when Green Line services were withdrawn, no regular services were worked from Tunbridge Wells (TW) garage, and Romford (RF) was in service as a factory. With reinstatement of the Green Line services, operational duties were resumed by Tunbridge Wells, but Romford (RF) has remained out of service

*   *   *

Due to the growth of the bus fleet, there is an acute shortage of garage space ; some 750 buses have to be parked in the open street at night.

Negotiations are completed for land purchase and building plans prepared for new London accommodation, but the financial crisis has caused a postponement of construction, together with plans for alterations and extensions to accommodate the buses which are to replace the South London trams.

CLASSIFIED NUMERICAL LIST
OF VEHICLES

| LT Class | | | | | | | | | |

A vehicle whose number does not appear
is no longer in service.
† Indicates vehicle to be withdrawn.

1	63	118	175	225	267	310	355	399
2	66	119	177	226	268	311	356	400
5	67	120	178	227	269	312	358	401
8	68	122	180	228	270	313	359	402
11	70	123	182	230	271	315	360	403
12	71	124	183	231	272	316	361	404
13	72	125	185	232	273	317	362	405
14	73	128†	187	233	274	318	364	408
16	74	129	188	234	275	319	365	409
18†	78	131	190	235	277	320	366	411
19	80	132	191	236	278	322	367	412
20	81	134	194	237	279	323	368	413
24	83	135†	195	238	280	324	369	414
26	85	138	196	239	281	325	370	416†
27	86	141†	197	240	282	326	372	418
31	88	144	198	243	283	327	373	419
33	90	145	199	244	284	328	374	420
34	91	147	200	245	285	329	375	421
35	93	148	202	247	287	330	376	422
36	94†	149	203	248	289	332	377	423†
37	96	152	204	249	290	334	379	424
38	97	153	205	250	291	336	380	425
39	99	156	206	251	292	337	381	426
40	102	158	207	252	293	338	382	427
42	103	159	208†	253	294	339	383	428
45	104	161	210	255	295	340	384	429
46	105	162	212	256	296	343	385	430
48	106	163	215	258	301	344	387	431
50	107	165	216	259	302	346	388	432
52	108	167	218	261	303	347	390	433
53	110	168	219	262	304	349	391	434
54	112	169	220	263	305	351†	392	435
58†	113	171	221	264	306	352	394	438
59	116†	173	222	265	307	353	395	439
60	117†	174	223	266	308	354	398	440

441	493	542	591	639	686	736	787	843
442	494	543	593	640	687	737	788	845
443	495	544	594	641	688	738	790	846
444	496	545	595	642	689	739	791	847
446	497	546	596	643	692	740	792	848
447	498	547	597	644	693	741	794	850
448	499	549	598	645	694	742	797	851
449	500	550	599	646	695	743	798	852
450	502	554	601	648	696	744	799	853
452	503	555	602	649	697	747	801	854
453	504	556	603	650	698	748	802	855
454	505	557	605	652	699	749	803	857
455	506	558	606	653	700	750	805	858
456	507	559	607	654	702	751	806	859
457	508	560	608	655	703	752	807	860
458	510	561	609	656	704	753	809	861
459	512	562	610	657	706	754	811	862
460	513	563	611	658	707	755	812	863
462	514	564	612	659	708	757	813	864
463	515	565	613	660	709	758	814	865
464	516	566	614	661	710	759	815	867
465	517	567	615	663	711	760	816	868
467	518	568	616	664	712	761	819	870
468	519	569	617	665	713	762	820	871
469	520	570	618	666	714	763	821†	872
470	521	571	619	667	715	764	822	873
471	522	572	620	668	716	765	823	874
472	523	573	621	669	717	766	824†	875
473	524	574	622	670†	718	767	825	876
474	525	575	623	671	719†	768	826	877
476	526	576	624	672	720	769	827	879
477	527	577	625	673	722	770	828	880
479	528	578	626	674	723	772	829	881
481	530	579	627	675	724	775	830	882
482†	531	580	628	676	725	776	831	883
483	533	582	629	677	726	777	832	884
485	534	583	630	678	727	778	833	885
487	535	584	632	679	728	779	836	886
488	536	585	633	680	729	780	837	887
489	537	586	634	681	730	781	838	888
490	538	587	635	682	731	782	840	889
491	539†	588	636	684	733	783	841	890
492	541	589	638	685	734	784	842	891†

892	937	986	1036	1085	1129	1175	1225	1280
893	938	987	1037	1086	1130	1176	1226	1281
894	939	988	1040	1087	1131	1177	1227	1282
895	940	990	1041	1089	1132	1178	1229	1283
896	941	992	1042	1090	1133	1179	1230	1284
897	942	993	1043	1091	1134	1180	1231	1285
898	943	995	1044	1092	1135	1181	1232	1287
899	945	996	1045	1093	1136	1182	1233	1288
900	946	997	1046	1094	1138	1183	1235	1289
901	947	998	1047	1095	1139	1184	1236	1290
902	948	999	1048	1096	1140	1185	1237	1291
903	949	1001	1049	1097	1141	1186	1238	1292
904	950	1002	1050	1098	1142	1187	1239	1294
905	951	1003	1052	1099	1143	1188	1241	1295
906	952	1004	1053	1100	1144	1189	1243	1296
907	953	1005	1055	1101	1145	1190	1244	1297
908	954	1006	1056	1102	1147	1191	1246	1298
909	955	1007	1057	1103	1148	1192	1247	1299
910	957	1008	1058	1104	1149	1193	1248	1301
911	959	1009	1059	1105	1150	1194	1249	1302
912	960	1010	1060	1106	1152	1195	1251†	1303
913	961	1011	1061	1107	1153	1196	1252	1304
914	963	1012	1062	1108	1154	1197	1254	1305
916	964	1013	1063	1109	1155	1198	1255	1306†
917	965	1014	1064	1110	1156	1199	1256	1307
918	966	1015	1065	1111	1157	1200	1258	1310
919	967	1016	1066	1112	1158	1201	1259	1311
920	968†	1017	1067	1113	1159	1204	1261	1312
921	969	1018	1068	1114	1160	1205	1262	1314
922	970	1019	1069	1115	1161	1206	1263	1315
923	971	1022	1071	1116	1162	1207	1266	1316
924	972	1023	1072	1117	1163	1208†	1267	1317
925	973	1024	1073	1118	1164	1209	1269	1318
926	975	1025	1074	1119	1165	1210	1270	1319
927	976	1026	1075	1120	1166	1212	1271	1320†
929	977	1027	1076	1121	1167	1213	1272	1321
930	978	1028	1077	1122	1168	1216	1273	1323
931	980	1029	1078	1123	1169	1217	1274	1324
932	981	1030	1079	1124	1170	1218	1275	1325
933	982	1031	1080	1125	1171	1219	1276	1326
934	983	1033	1081	1126	1172	1221	1277	1328
935	984	1034	1082	1127	1173	1222	1278	1329
936	985	1035	1083	1128	1174	1224	1279	1330

1331	1341	1354	1364†	1375	1386	1397	1409	1420
1332	1343	1355	1365	1376	1387	1398	1410	1421
1333	1344†	1356	1366	1378	1389	1399	1411	1422
1334	1345	1357	1368†	1379	1390	1400	1412	1423
1335	1346	1358	1369	1380	1391	1401	1414	1424
1336	1347	1359	1370†	1381	1392	1402	1415	1425
1337	1348	1360	1371	1382	1393	1403	1416	1426
1338	1349	1361	1372	1383	1394	1404	1417	1427
1339	1350	1362	1373	1384	1395	1406	1418	1428
1340	1351	1363	1374	1385	1396	1407	1419	

ST Class

ST 1-305

1	37	72	103	137	168	201	236	270	
2	38	73	104	138	169	202	237	271	
3	39	74	106	139	170	204	238	273	
4	42	75	107	140†	172	205	240	274	
5	43	76	108	141	173	207	241	275	
9	45	77	109	142	174	208	242	276	
10	47	78	110	143	175	209	243	277	
11	48	79	111	144	176	210	244	279	
13	49	80	113	145	177	211†	245	280	
14	50	81	114	146	178	212	246	281	
15	51	82	115	147	179	214	248	283	
16	52	83	116	148	180†	215	249	284	
17	53	84	117	149	181	216	250	285	
18	55	85	119	150†	182	218	251	286	
19	56	86	122	152	183	219	252	288	
21	58	87	123	153	184	220	253	289	
22	59	88	124	154	185	221	254	290	
23	60	89	125	155	186	222	256	291	
25	61	90	126	157	189	224	257	293	
26	62	91	127	158	190	225	258	294	
27	63	93	128	159	191	226	259	295	
29	64	94†	129	160	192	227	261	296	
30	65	95	130	161	193	228†	262	297	
31	66	96	131	162	194	229	263	298	
32	67	97	132	163	195	230	264	300	
33	68	99	133	164	196	231	265	301	
34	69	100	134	165	197	232	266	302	
35	70	101	135	166	199	233	267	303	
36	71	102	136	167	200	234	268	305	

306	354	402	454	497	546	595	641	692
307	355	403	455	498	547	596	642	693
308	356	404	456	499	548	597	643	694
309	357	405	457	501	549	598	645	695
310	358	406	458	502	550	599	646	696
311	359	408	459	503	551	601	648	697
312	360	409	460	504	552	603	649	698
313	361	410	461	505	553†	605	650	699
314†	362	412	462	506†	554	606	651	700
315	363	413	463	507	555	607	652	701
316	364	414	464	508	557	608	653	702
317	366	415	465	509	558	609	654	703
318	368	416	466	510	559	610	655	704
319	369	417	467†	511	561	611	656	705
320†	370	418	468	512	562	612	658	706
321	371	419	469	513	564	613	659	707
323	372	420	470	514	566	614	660	708
324	373	421	471	515	567	615	661	709
325	374	424	472	517†	568	616	662	710
326	375	425	473	518	569	617	663	711
327	376	426	474	519	572	618	664	712
328	377	427	475	520	573	619	665	713
331	378	428	476	521	574	620	666	715
332	379	430†	477	522	575	621†	667	716
333	380	431	478	524	576	622	668	717
334	382	432	479	525	577	623	669	718
335	383	433	480	527	578	624	670	719
336	384	434	481	528	579†	625	671	722
338	385	435	482	529	580	626	672	723†
339	386	436	483	530	581	627	674	724
340	387	437	484	531	582	628	676	725
341	388	438	485	532	583	629	677	726
342	389	440	486	533	584	630	679	727
344	390	442	487	534	585	631	680	728
345	391	443	488	535	586	632†	682	729
346	393	444	489	536	587	633	683	730
347	394†	445	490	537	588	634	685	731
348	395	447	491	538	589	635	686	732
349	396	448	492	539	590	636	687	733
350	398	449	493†	540	591†	637	688	734
351	399	451	494	542	592	638	689	735
352	400	452	495	543	593	639†	690	736
353	401	453	496	544	594	640	691	737

738	769	804	835	905	981†	1046	1077	1110
740	770	806	836†	906	983	1047	1078	1111
741	773	807	838	910	988	1048	1079	1112
742	774	808	842	914	989	1049	1080	1114
743	775	809	843	918	993	1050	1081†	1115
744	776	810†	844	920	994	1052†	1083	1116
745	778	811	848	921	998	1053	1084	1117
746	779	812	849	925	1011	1054	1085	1118
747	781	813	850	926	1020	1055	1086	1119
748	782	814	855	928	1022	1056	1089	1120
749	783	815	856	931	1023	1057	1090	1121
750	784	816	860	935	1024	1058	1091	1122
751	785	817	861	939	1025	1059	1092	1124
752	786	818	864	941	1026	1060	1093	1125
753	787	819	866	942	1027	1061	1094	1126
754	790†	820	868	944	1032†	1062	1095	1127
756	791	821	872	945	1033	1063	1096	1128
757	792	822	877	947	1034	1064	1097	1129
758	793†	824	880	957	1035†	1065	1098	1130
759	794	825	882	959	1036	1066†	1109	1131
760	795	826	883	962†	1037†	1067	1100	1132
761	796	827	884	963†	1039	1068	1101	1133
762	797	828	885	964†	1040	1069	1103	1134
763	799†	829	887	970	1041	1070	1104	1135
764	800	830	891	971†	1042	1073	1105	1136
765	801	831	894	972	1043	1074	1106	1137
766	802	833	896	975	1044	1075	1108	1138
767	803†	834	899†	979	1045	1076	1109	1139
768†								

T Class   T 1-239

1	8	16	27	36	44	156	215	231
2	9	17	28	37	45	207	216	232
3	10	18	30	39	46	208	219	234
4	11	20	31	40	47	209	223	236
5	12	22	32	41	48	212	226	237
6	13	23	33	42	49	213	229	238
7	14	24	34	43	50	214	230	239

244	364	442	489	533	577	623	668	713
249	369	444	490	534	578	624	669	714
250	391	445	491	535	579	625	671	715
251	396	446	492	536	580	626	672	716
252	403	447	493	537	581	627	673	717
253	404	448	494	538	582	628	674	718
255	405	449	495	539	583	629	675	719
261	406	450	496	540	584	630	676	720
262	407	451	497	541	585	631	677	721
264	408	452	498	542	588	632	678	722
265	409	453	499	543	589	633	679	723
267	410	454	500	544	590	634	680	724
270	411	455	501	545	591	635	682	725
271	412	456	502	546	592	636	683	726
273	413	457	503	547	593	637	684	727
275	414	458	504	548	595	638	685	728
276	415	459	505	549	596	639	686	729
277	416	461	506	550	597	640	687	730
280	417	462	507	551	598	641	688	731
283	418	463	508	552	599	642	689	732
285	419	464	510	553	600	643	690	733
290	420	465	511	554	601	644	691	734
292	421	466	512	555	602	645	692	735
296	422	467	513	556	603	646	693	736
297	423	468	514	557	604	647	694	737
298	424	469	515	558	605	648	695	738
301	425	470	516	559	606	649	696	739
302	426	471	517	560	607	650	697	740
307	427	472	518	561	608	651	698	741
308	428	473	519	562	609	652	699	742
309	429	474	520	563	610	653	700	743
310	430	475	521	564	611	654	701	744
311	431	476	522	565	612	655	702	745
312	432	477	523	566	613	656	703	746
313	433	478	524	567	614	657	704	747
314	434	479	525	568	615	658	705	748
315	435	480	526	569	616	659	706	749
316	436	481	527	570	617	660	707	750
317	437	482	528	571	618	661	708	751
318	438	483	529	572	619	662	709	752
359	439	484	530	574	620	663	710	753
361	440	485	531	575	621	664	711	754
362	441	487	532	576	622	667	712	755

756	761	766	771	776	781	786	791	795
757	762	767	772	777	782	787	792	796
758	763	768	773	778	783	788	793	797
759	764	769	774	779	784	789	794	798
760	765	770	775	780	785	790		

STL Class   STL 1-343

1	45	85	*140*	175	212	243	274	306
3	46†	86	*141*	176	213	244	275	307
4	47	89	*142*	178	214	245	276	308
5	48	91†	*143*	179	215	246	277	309
6	49	92	*144*	180†	216	247	278	310
8†	50	95	*145*	181	217	248	279	311
9†	52	102	*146*	182	218	249	280	312
10	54	103	*147*	183†	219	250	281	313
12†	55	108	*148*	185	220	251	282	314†
14	56	111	*149*	188	221	252	283	316
15	57	113†	*150*	189†	222	253	284	317
16	58	115	*151*	190†	223	254	285	318
17	59	117	*152*	191	224	255	286	319
19†	60	118	153	192†	225	256	287	320†
20	61	119	154†	194	226	257	288	321
21†	62	121	155	195	227	258	289	322
22†	64	122†	157	197	228	259	290	323†
24†	65	123	158	198	229	260	291	324
25	67	124	159†	199	230	261	292	325
28	68	125	160	200	231	262	293	329†
30†	69	126	162	201	232	263	294†	330†
31†	70	128	163	202	233	264	295	332†
33	72	*131*	164	203	234	265	296	333
34	73	*132*	165	204	235	266	297†	334
35	74	*133*	166	205	236	267	298	335
37	75	*134*	167	206	237	268	299	337
38†	76	*135*	168	207	238	269	300	339
39	78	*136*	169	208	239	270	301	341
40†	81	*137*	171	209	240	271	303	342
42†	83	*138*	172	210	241	272	304	343
43	84	*139*	174	211	242	273		

Figures in italics denote numbers not allocated.

344	408	451	494	537	582	625	668	711
345	409	452	495	538	583	626	669	712
346	410	453	496	539	584	627	670	713
347	411	454	497	540	585	628	671	714
348	412	455	498	541	586	629	672	715
349	413	456	499	542	587	630	673	716
350	414	457	500	543	588	631	674	717
351	415	358	501	544	589	632	675	718
352	416	459	502	545	590	633	676	719
353	417	460	503	546	591	634	677	720
354	418	461	504	547	592	635	678	721
356	419	462	505	548	593	636	679	722
357	420	463	506	549	594	637	680	723
359	421	464	507	550	595	638	681	724
360	422	465	508	551	596	639	682	725
361	423	466	509	552	597	640	683	726
362	424	467	510	553	598	641	684	727
369	425	468	511	555	599	642	685	728
370	426	469	512	556	600	643	686	729
371	427	470	513	557	601	644	687	730
372	428	471	514	559	602	645	688	731
373	429	472	515	560	603	646	689	732
374	430	473	516	561	604	647	690	733
375	431	474	517	562	605	648	691	734
376	432	475	518	563	606	649	692	735
377	433	476	519	564	607	650	693	736
379	434	477	520	565	608	651	694	737
381	435	478	521	566	609	652	695	738
382	436	479	522	567	610	653	696	739
383	437	480	523	568	611	654	697	740
384	438	481	524	569	612	655	698	741
386	439	482	525	570	613	656	699	742
387	440	483	526	571	614	657	700	743
388	441	484	527	572	615	658	701	744
390†	442	485	528	573	616	659	702	746
396	443	486	529	574	617	660	703	747
397	444	487	530	575	618	661	704	748
401†	445	488	531	576	619	662	705	749
403	446	489	532	577	620	663	706	750
404	447	490	533	578	621	664	707	751
405	448	491	534	579	622	665	708	752
406	449	492	535	580	623	666	709	753
407	450	493	536	581	624	667	710	754

755	799	842	885	928	971	1014	1057	1100
756	800	843	886	929	972	1015	1058	1101
757	801	844	887	930	973	1016	1059	1102
758	802	845	888	931	974	1017	1060	1103
759	803	846	889	932	975	1018	1061	1104
760	804	847	890	933	976	1019	1062	1105
761	805	848	891	934	977	1020	1063	1106
762	806	849	892	935	978	1021	1064	1107
763	807	850	893	936	979	1022	1065	1108
764	808	851	894	937	980	1023	1066	1109
765	809	852	895	938	981	1024	1067	1110
766	810	853	896	939	982	1025	1068	1111
767	811	854	897	940	983	1026	1069	1112
768	812	855	898	941	984	1027	1070	1113
769	813	856	899	942	985	1028	1071	1114
770	814	857	900	943	986	1029	1072	1115
771	815	858	901	944	987	1030	1073	1116
772	816	859	902	945	988	1031	1074	1117
773	817	860	903	946	989	1032	1075	1118
774	818	861	904	947	990	1033	1076	1119
775	819	862	905	948	991	1034	1077	1120
776	820	863	906	949	992	1035	1078	1121
777	821	864	907	950	993	1036	1079	1122
778	822	865	908	951	994	1037	1080	1123
779	823	866	909	952	995	1038	1081	1124
780	824	867	910	953	996	1039	1082	1125
781	825	868	911	954	997	1040	1083	1126
783	826	869	912	955	998	1041	1084	1127
784	827	870	913	956	999	1042	1085	1128
785	828	871	814	957	1000	1043	1086	1129
786	829	872	915	958	1001	1044	1087	1130
787	830	873	816	959	1002	1045	1088	1131
788	831	874	917	960	1003	1046	1089	1132
789	832	875	918	961	1004	1047	1090	1133
790	833	876	919	962	1005	1048	1091	1134
791	834	877	920	963	1006	1049	1092	1135
792	835	878	921	964	1007	1050	1093	1136
793	836	879	922	965	1008	1051	1094	1137
794	837	880	923	966	1009	1052	1095	1138
795	838	881	924	967	1010	1053	1096	1139
796	839	882	925	968	1011	1054	1097	1140
797	840	883	926	969	1012	1055	1098	1141
798	841	884	927	970	1013	1056	1099	1142

1143	1186	1229	1272	1315	1358	1402	1445	1488
1144	1187	1230	1273	1316	1359	1403	1446	1489
1145	1188	1231	1274	1317	1360	1404	1447	1490
1146	1189	1232	1275	1318	1361	1405	1448	1491
1147	1190	1233	1276	1319	1362	1406	1449	1492
1148	1191	1234	1277	1320	1363	1407	1450	1493
1149	1192	1235	1278	1321	1364	1408	1451	1494
1150	1193	1236	1279	1322	1365	1409	1452	1495
1151	1194	1237	1280	1323	1366	1410	1453	1496
1152	1195	1238	1281	1324	1367	1411	1454	1497
1153	1196	1239	1282	1325	1368	1412	1455	1498
1154	1197	1240	1283	1326	1369	1413	1456	1499
1155	1198	1241	1284	1327	1370	1414	1457	1500
1156	1199	1242	1285	1328	1371	1415	1458	1501
1157	1200	1243	1286	1329	1372	1416	1459	1502
1158	1201	1244	1287	1330	1373	1417	1460	1503
1159	1202	1245	1288	1331	1374	1418	1461	1504
1160	1203	1246	1289	1332	1375	1419	1462	1505
1161	1204	1247	1290	1333	1376	1420	1463	1506
1162	1205	1248	1291	1334	1377	1421	1464	1507
1163	1206	1249	1292	1335	1378	1422	1465	1508
1164	1207	1250	1293	1336	1379	1423	1466	1509
1165	1208	1251	1294	1337	1380	1424	1467	1510
1166	1209	1252	1295	1338	1381	1425	1468	1511
1167	1210	1253	1296	1339	1382	1426	1469	1512
1168	1211	1254	1297	1340	1383	1427	1470	1513
1169	1212	1255	1298	1341	1384	1428	1471	1514
1170	1213	1256	1299	1342	1385	1429	1472	1515
1171	1214	1257	1300	1343	1387	1430	1473	1516
1172	1215	1258	1301	1344	1388	1431	1474	1517
1173	1216	1259	1302	1345	1389	1432	1475	1518
1174	1217	1260	1303	1346	1390	1433	1476	1519
1175	1218	1261	1304	1347	1391	1434	1477	1520
1176	1219	1262	1305	1348	1392	1435	1478	1521
1177	1220	1263	1306	1349	1393	1436	1479	1522
1178	1221	1264	1307	1350	1394	1437	1480	1523
1179	1222	1265	1308	1351	1395	1438	1481	1524
1180	1223	1266	1309	1352	1396	1439	1482	1525
1181	1224	1267	1310	1353	1397	1440	1483	1526
1182	1225	1268	1311	1354	1398	1441	1484	1527
1183	1226	1269	1312	1355	1399	1442	1485	1528
1184	1227	1270	1313	1356	1400	1443	1486	1529
1185	1228	1271	1314	1357	1401	1444	1487	1530

1531	1574	1617	1660	1703	1746	1789	1832	1875
1532	1575	1618	1661	1704	1747	1790	1833	1876
1533	1576	1619	1662	1705	1748	1791	1834	1877
1534	1577	1620	1663	1706	1749	1792	1835	1878
1535	1578	1621	1664	1707	1750	1793	1836	1879
1536	1579	1622	1665	1708	1751	1794	1837	1880
1537	1580	1623	1666	1709	1752	1795	1838	1881
1538	1581	1624	1667	1710	1753	1796	1839	1882
1539	1582	1625	1668	1711	1754	1797	1840	1883
1540	1583	1626	1669	1712	1755	1798	1841	1884
1541	1584	1627	1670	1713	1756	1799	1842	1885
1542	1585	1628	1671	1714	1757	1800	1843	1886
1543	1586	1629	1672	1715	1758	1801	1844	1887
1544	1587	1630	1673	1716	1759	1802	1845	1888
1545	1588	1631	1674	1717	1760	1803	1846	1889
1546	1589	1632	1675	1718	1761	1804	1847	1890
1547	1590	1633	1676	1719	1762	1805	1848	1891
1548	1591	1634	1677	1720	1763	1806	1849	1892
1549	1592	1635	1678	1721	1764	1807	1850	1893
1550	1593	1636	1679	1722	1765	1808	1851	1894
1551	1594	1637	1680	1723	1766	1809	1852	1895
1552	1595	1638	1681	1724	1767	1810	1853	1896
1553	1596	1639	1682	1725	1768	1811	1854	1897
1554	1597	1640	1683	1726	1769	1812	1855	1898
1555	1598	1641	1684	1727	1770	1813	1856	1899
1556	1599	1642	1685	1728	1771	1814	1857	1900
1557	1600	1643	1686	1729	1772	1815	1858	1901
1558	1601	1644	1687	1730	1773	1816	1859	1902
1559	1602	1645	1688	1731	1774	1817	1860	1903
1560	1603	1646	1689	1732	1775	1818	1861	1904
1561	1604	1647	1690	1733	1776	1819	1862	1905
1562	1605	1648	1691	1734	1777	1820	1863	1906
1563	1606	1649	1692	1735	1778	1821	1864	1907
1564	1607	1650	1693	1736	1779	1822	1865	1908
1565	1608	1651	1694	1737	1780	1823	1866	1909
1566	1609	1652	1695	1738	1781	1824	1867	1910
1567	1610	1653	1696	1739	1782	1825	1868	1911
1568	1611	1654	1697	1740	1783	1826	1869	1912
1569	1612	1655	1698	1741	1784	1827	1870	1913
1570	1613	1656	1699	1742	1785	1828	1871	1914
1571	1614	1657	1700	1743	1786	1829	1872	1915
1572	1615	1658	1701	1744	1787	1830	1873	1916
1573	1616	1659	1702	1745	1788	1831	1874	1917

1918	1961	2004	2048	2091	2134	2177	2220	2263
1919	1962	2005	2049	2092	2135	2178	2221	2264
1920	1963	2006	2050	2093	2136	2179	2222	2265
1921	1964	2007	2051	2094	2137	2180	2223	2266
1922	1965	2008	2052	2095	2138	2181	2224	2267
1923	1966	2009	2053	2096	2139	2182	2225	2268
1924	1967	2010	2054	2097	2140	2183	2226	2269
1925	1968	2011	2055	2098	2141	2184	2227	2270
1926	1969	2012	2056	2099	2142	2185	2228	2271
1927	1970	2013	2057	2100	2143	2186	2229	2272
1928	1971	2014	2058	2101	2144	2187	2230	2273
1929	1972	2015	2059	2102	2145	2188	2231	2274
1930	1973	2016	2060	2103	2146	2189	2232	2275
1931	1974	2017	2061	2104	2147	2190	2233	2276
1932	1975	2018	2062	2105	2148	2191	2234	2277
1933	1976	2019	2063	2106	2149	2192	2235	2278
1934	1977	2020	2064	2107	2150	2193	2236	2279
1935	1978	2021	2065	2108	2151	2194	2237	2280
1936	1979	2022	2066	2109	2152	2195	2238	2281
1937	1980	2023	2067	2110	2153	2196	2239	2282
1938	1981	2024	2068	2111	2154	2197	2240	2283
1939	1982	2025	2069	2112	2155	2198	2241	2284
1940	1983	2026	2070	2113	2156	2199	2242	2285
1941	1984	2027	2071	2114	2157	2200	2243	2286
1942	1985	2028	2072	2115	2158	2201	2244	2287
1943	1986	2029	2073	2116	2159	2202	2245	2288
1944	1987	2030	2074	2117	2160	2203	2246	2289
1945	1988	2031	2075	2118	2161	2204	2247	2290
1946	1989	2032	2076	2119	2162	2205	2248	2291
1947	1990	2033	2077	2120	2163	2206	2249	2292
1948	1991	2034	2078	2121	2164	2207	2250	2293
1949	1992	2035	2079	2122	2165	2208	2251	2294
1950	1993	2036	2080	2123	2166	2209	2252	2295
1951	1994	2037	2081	2124	2167	2210	2253	2296
1952	1995	2038	2082	2125	2168	2211	2254	2297
1953	1996	2039	2083	2126	2169	2212	2255	2298
1954	1997	2040	2084	2127	2170	2213	2256	2299
1955	1998	2041	2085	2128	2171	2214	2257	2300
1956	1999	2042	2086	2129	2172	2215	2258	2301
1957	2000	2043	2087	2130	2173	2216	2259	2302
1958	2001	2044	2088	2131	2174	2217	2260	2303
1959	2002	2045	2089	2132	2175	2218	2261	2304
1960	2003	2047	2090	2133	2176	2219	2262	2305

STL 2696.   Post-war Country vehicle,
with MCW coachwork.

STL's 1357 and 2629.   The rear vehicle has route number indicator in roof

[*B. V. Franey*

STL 70 : One of the Tilling type.   [F. G. Reynolds

RTL 501

TWO TYPES OF COACH

LTC 17

TF 68

[B. V. Franey

TF 7c : One of the coaches used on sight-seeing tours.

D 140 : Daimler CWD 6 with Duple body. [S. L. Poole

2306	2350	2394	2440	2484	2528	2572	2616	2660
2307	2351	2395	2441	2485	2529	2573	2617	2661
2308	2352	2396	2442	2486	2530	2574	2618	2662
2309	2353	2397	2443	2487	2531	2575	2619	2663
2310	2354	2398	2444	2488	2532	2576	2620	2664
2311	2355	2399	2445	2489	2533	2577	2621	2665
2312	2356	2400	2446	2490	2534	2578	2622	2666
2313	2357	2401	2447	2491	2535	2579	2623	2667
2314	2358	2402	2448	2492	2536	2580	2624	2668
2315	2359	2403	2449	2493	2537	2581	2625	2669
2316	2360	2404	2450	2494	2538	2582	2626	2670
2317	2361	2405	2451	2495	2539	2583	2627	2671
2318	2362	2406	2452	2496	2540	2584	2628	2672
2319	2363	2407	2453	2497	2541	2585	2629	2673
2320	2364	2408	2454	2498	2542	2586	2630	2674
2321	2365	2409	2455	2499	2543	2587	2631	2675
2322	2366	2410	2456	2500	2544	2588	2632	2676
2323	2367	2411	2457	2501	2545	2589	2633	2677
2324	2368	2412	2458	2502	2546	2590	2634	2678
2325	2369	2413	2459	2503	2547	2591	2635	2679
2326	2370	2414	2460	2504	2548	2592	2636	2680
2327	2371	2415	2461	2505	2549	2593	2637	2681
2328	2372	2416	2462	2506	2550	2594	2638	2682
2329	2373	2417	2463	2507	2551	2595	2639	2683
2330	2374	2419	2464	2508	2552	2596	2640	2684
2331	2375	2420	2465	2509	2553	2597	2641	2685
2332	2376	2421	2466	2510	2554	2598	2642	2686
2333	2377	2422	2467	2511	2555	2599	2643	2687
2334	2378	2423	2468	2512	2556	2600	2644	2688
2335	2379	2425	2469	2513	2557	2601	2645	2689
2336	2380	2426	2470	2514	2558	2602	2646	2690
2337	2381	2427	2471	2515	2559	2603	2647	2691
2338	2382	2428	2472	2516	2560	2604	2648	2692
2339	2383	2429	2473	2517	2561	2605	2649	2693
2340	2384	2430	2474	2518	2562	2606	2650	2694
2341	2385	2431	2475	2519	2563	2607	2651	2695
2342	2386	2432	2476	2520	2564	2608	2652	2696
2343	2387	2433	2477	2521	2565	2609	2653	2697
2344	2388	2434	2478	2522	2566	2610	2654	2698
2345	2389	2435	2479	2523	2567	2611	2655	2699
2346	2390	2436	2480	2524	2568	2612	2656	2700
2347	2391	2437	2481	2525	2569	2613	2657	2701
2348	2392	2438	2482	2526	2570	2614	2658	
2349	2393	2439	2483	2527	2571	2615	2659	

1	33	65	97	129	161	193	225	257
2	34	66	98	130	162	194	226	258
3	35	67	99	131	163	195	227	259
4	36	68	100	132	164	196	228	260
5	37	69	101	133	165	197	229	261
6	38	70	102	134	166	198	230	262
7	39	71	103	135	167	199	231	263
8	40	72	104	136	168	200	232	264
9	41	73	105	137	169	201	233	265
10	42	74	106	138	170	202	234	266
11	43	75	107	139	171	203	235	267
12	44	76	108	140	172	204	236	268
13	45	77	109	141	173	205	237	269
14	46	78	110	142	174	206	238	270
15	47	79	111	143	175	207	239	271
16	48	80	112	144	176	208	240	272
17	49	81	113	145	177	209	241	273
18	50	82	114	146	178	210	242	274
19	51	83	115	147	179	211	243	275
20	52	84	116	148	180	212	244	276
21	53	85	117	149	181	213	245	277
22	54	86	118	150	182	214	246	278
23	55	87	119	151	183	215	247	279
24	56	88	120	152	184	216	248	280
25	57	89	121	153	185	217	249	281
26	58	90	122	154	186	218	250	
27	59	91	123	155	187	219	251	
28	60	92	124	156	188	220	252	
29	61	93	125	157	189	221	253	
30	62	94	126	158	190	222	254	
31	63	95	127	159	191	223	255	
32	64	96	128	160	192	224	256	

1	7	13	19	25	31	37	43	49
2	8	14	20	26	32	38	44	50
3	9	15	21	27	33	39	45	51
4	10	16	22	28	34	40	46	52
5	11	17	23	29	35	41	47	53
6	12	18	24	30	36	42	48	54

55	98	141	184	227	270	313	356	399
56	99	142	185	228	271	314	357	400
57	100	143	186	229	272	315	358	401
58	101	144	187	230	273	316	359	402
59	102	145	188	231	274	317	360	403
60	103	146	189	232	275	318	361	404
61	104	147	190	233	276	319	362	405
62	105	148	191	234	277	320	363	406
63	106	149	192	235	278	321	364	407
64	107	150	193	236	279	322	365	408
65	108	151	194	237	280	323	366	409
66	109	152	195	238	281	324	367	410
67	110	153	196	239	282	325	368	411
68	111	154	197	240	283	326	369	412
69	112	155	198	241	284	327	370	413
70	113	156	199	242	285	328	371	414
71	114	157	200	243	286	329	372	415
72	115	158	201	244	287	330	373	416
73	116	159	202	245	288	331	374	417
74	117	160	203	246	289	332	375	418
75	118	161	204	247	290	333	376	419
76	119	162	205	248	291	334	377	420
77	120	163	206	249	292	335	378	421
78	121	164	207	250	293	336	379	422
79	122	165	208	251	294	337	380	423
80	123	166	209	252	295	338	381	424
81	124	167	210	253	296	339	382	425
82	125	168	211	254	297	340	383	426
83	126	169	212	255	298	341	384	427
84	127	170	213	256	299	342	385	428
85	128	171	214	257	300	343	386	429
86	129	172	215	258	301	344	387	430
87	130	173	216	259	302	345	388	431
88	131	174	217	260	303	346	309	432
89	132	175	218	261	304	347	390	433
90	133	176	219	262	305	348	391	434
91	134	177	220	263	306	349	392	435
92	135	178	221	264	307	350	393	
93	136	179	222	265	308	351	394	
94	137	180	223	266	309	352	395	
95	138	181	224	267	310	353	396	
96	139	182	225	268	311	354	397	
97	140	183	226	269	312	355	398	

B Class

1	4	7	10	13	16	19	22	26
2	5	8	11	14	17	20	23	27
3	6	9	12	15	18	21	24	28
							25	29

RT Class

2	35	68	101	134	167	200	233	266
3	36	69	102	135	168	201	234	267
4	37	70	103	136	169	202	235	268
5	38	71	104	137	170	203	236	269
6	39	72	105	138	171	204	237	270
7	40	73	106	139	172	205	238	271
8	41	74	107	140	173	206	239	272
9	42	75	108	141	174	207	240	273
10	43	76	109	142	175	208	241	274
11	44	77	110	143	176	209	242	275
12	45	78	111	144	177	210	243	276
13	46	79	112	145	178	211	244	277
14	47	80	113	146	179	212	245	278
15	48	81	114	147	180	213	246	279
16	49	82	115	148	181	214	247	280
17	50	83	116	149	182	215	248	281
18	51	84	117	150	183	216	249	282
19	52	85	118	151	184	217	250	283
20	53	86	119	152	185	218	251	284
21	54	87	120	153	186	219	252	285
22	55	88	121	154	187	220	253	286
23	56	89	122	155	188	221	254	287
24	57	90	123	156	189	222	255	288
25	58	91	124	157	190	223	256	289
26	59	92	125	158	191	224	257	290
27	60	93	126	159	192	225	258	291
28	61	94	127	160	193	226	259	292
29	62	95	128	161	194	227	260	293
30	63	96	129	162	195	228	261	294
31	64	97	130	163	196	229	262	295
32	65	98	131	164	197	230	263	296
33	66	99	132	165	198	231	264	297
34	67	100	133	166	199	232	265	298

299	342	385	428	471	514	557	600	643
300	343	386	429	472	515	558	601	644
301	344	387	430	473	516	559	602	645
302	345	388	431	474	517	560	603	646
303	346	389	432	475	518	561	604	647
304	347	390	433	476	519	562	605	648
305	348	391	434	477	520	563	606	649
306	349	392	435	478	521	564	607	650
307	350	393	436	479	522	565	608	651
308	351	394	437	480	523	566	609	652
309	352	395	438	481	524	567	610	653
310	353	396	439	482	525	568	611	654
311	354	397	440	483	526	569	612	655
312	355	398	441	484	527	570	613	656
313	356	399	442	485	528	571	614	657
314	357	400	443	486	529	572	615	658
315	358	401	444	487	530	573	616	659
316	359	402	445	488	531	574	617	660
317	360	403	446	489	532	575	618	661
318	361	404	447	490	533	576	619	662
319	362	405	448	491	534	577	620	663
320	363	406	449	492	535	578	621	664
321	364	407	450	493	536	579	622	665
322	365	408	451	494	537	580	623	666
323	366	409	452	495	538	581	624	667
324	367	410	453	496	539	582	625	668
325	368	411	454	497	540	583	626	669
326	369	412	455	498	541	584	627	670
327	370	413	456	499	542	585	628	671
328	371	414	457	500	543	586	629	672
329	372	415	458	501	544	587	630	673
330	373	416	459	502	545	588	631	674
331	374	417	460	503	546	589	632	675
332	375	418	461	504	547	590	633	676
333	376	419	462	505	548	591	634	677
334	377	420	463	506	549	592	635	678
335	378	421	464	507	550	593	636	679
336	379	422	465	508	551	594	637	680
337	380	423	466	509	552	595	638	681
338	381	424	467	510	553	596	639	682
339	382	425	468	511	554	597	640	683
340	383	426	469	512	555	598	641	684
341	384	427	470	513	556	599	642	685

686	722	758	794	830	866	902	938	974
687	723	759	795	831	867	903	939	975
688	724	760	796	832	868	904	940	976
689	725	761	797	833	869	905	941	977
690	726	762	798	834	870	906	942	978
691	727	763	799	835	871	907	943	979
692	728	764	800	836	872	908	944	980
693	729	765	801	837	873	909	945	981
694	730	766	802	838	874	910	946	982
695	731	767	803	839	875	911	947	983
696	732	768	804	840	876	912	948	984
697	733	769	805	841	877	913	949	985
698	734	770	806	842	878	914	950	986
699	735	771	807	843	879	915	951	987
700	736	772	808	844	880	916	952	988
701	737	773	809	845	881	917	953	989
702	738	774	810	846	882	918	954	990
703	739	775	811	847	883	919	955	991
704	740	776	812	848	884	920	956	992
705	741	777	813	849	885	921	957	993
706	742	778	814	850	886	922	958	994
707	743	779	815	851	887	923	959	995
708	744	780	816	852	888	924	960	996
709	745	781	817	853	889	925	961	997
710	746	782	818	854	890	926	962	998
711	747	783	819	855	891	927	963	999
712	748	784	820	856	892	928	964	1000
713	749	785	821	857	893	929	965	
714	750	786	822	858	894	930	966	
715	751	787	823	859	895	931	967	
716	752	788	824	860	896	832	968	
717	753	789	825	861	897	933	969	
718	754	790	826	862	898	934	970	
719	755	791	827	863	899	935	971	
720	756	792	828	864	900	936	972	
721	757	793	829	865	901	937	973	

STD Class

1	21	41	61	81	101	121	141	161
2	22	42	62	82	102	122	142	162
3	23	43	63	83	103	123	143	163
4	24	44	64	84	104	124	144	164
5	25	45	65	85	105	125	145	165
6	26	46	66	86	106	126	146	166
7	27	47	67	87	107	127	147	167
8	28	48	68	88	108	128	148	168
9	29	49	69	89	109	129	149	169
10	30	50	70	90	110	130	150	170
11	31	51	71	91	111	131	151	171
12	32	52	72	92	112	132	152	172
13	33	53	73	93	113	133	153	173
14	34	54	74	94	114	134	154	174
15	35	55	75	95	115	135	155	175
16	36	56	76	96	116	136	156	176
17	37	57	77	97	117	137	157	
18	38	58	78	98	118	138	158	
19	39	59	79	99	119	139	159	
20	40	60	80	100	120	140	160	

SINGLE DECK BUSES AND COACHES

C Class

2	16	25	37	47	59	70	90	106
3	17	26	38	49	60	73	91	107
4	18	28	39	50	61	74	92	108
7	19	30	40	52	63	77	93	109
8	20	31	41	53	64	78	94	110
11	21	32	42	56	65	81	95	111
13	22	34	44	57	66	82	97	112
14	23	36	43	58	69	88	98	113
15	24							

CR Class

1	7	13	20	25	30	35	40	45
2	8	14	21	26	31	36	41	46
3	9	15	22	27	32	37	42	47
4	10	16	23	28	33	38	43	48
5	11	17	24	29	34	39	44	49
6	12	19						

LTC Class

1	4	7	10	13	16	19	21	23
2	5	8	11	14	17	20	22	24
3	6	9	12	15	18			

Q CLASS

6	32	58	84	110	136	162	189	215
7	33	59	85	111	137	163	190	216
8	34	60	86	112	138	164	191	218
9	35	61	87	113	139	165	192	219
10	36	62	88	114	140	166	193	220
11	37	63	89	115	141	167	194	221
12	38	64	90	116	142	168	195	222
13	39	65	91	117	143	169	196	223
14	40	66	92	118	144	170	197	224
15	41	67	93	119	145	171	198	225
16	42	68	94	120	146	172	199	226
17	43	69	95	121	147	173	200	227
18	44	70	96	122	148	174	201	228
19	45	71	97	123	149	175	202	229
20	46	72	98	124	150	176	203	230
21	47	73	99	125	151	177	204	231
22	48	74	100	126	152	178	205	232
23	49	75	101	127	153	179	206	233
24	50	76	102	128	154	180	207	234
25	51	77	103	129	155	181	208	235
26	52	78	104	130	156	182	209	236
27	53	79	105	131	157	183	210	237
28	54	80	106	132	158	184	211	238
29	55	81	107	133	159	185	212	
30	56	82	108	134	160	186	213	
31	57	83	109	135	161	187	214	

TF Class

9	22	31	40	49	57	65	73	81
14	23	32	41	50	58	66	74	82
15	24	33	42	51	59	67	75	83
16	25	34	43	52	60	68	76	84
17	26	35	44	53	61	69	77	85
18	27	36	45	54	62	70	78	86
19	28	37	46	55	63	71	79	87
20	29	38	47	56	64	72	80	88
21	30	39	48					

TD Class

1	5	9	13	17	20	23	26	29
2	6	10	14	18	21	24	27	30
3	7	11	15	19	22	25	28	31
4	8	12	16					

DOUBLE DECK VEHICLES

RTL Class
Not yet in service

1	21	41	61	81	101	121	141	161
2	22	42	62	82	102	122	142	162
3	23	43	63	83	103	123	143	163
4	24	44	64	84	104	124	144	164
5	25	45	65	85	105	125	145	165
6	26	46	66	86	106	126	146	166
7	27	47	67	87	107	127	147	167
8	28	48	68	88	108	128	148	168
9	29	49	69	89	109	129	149	169
10	30	50	70	90	110	130	150	170
11	31	51	71	91	111	131	151	171
12	32	52	72	92	112	132	152	172
13	33	53	73	93	113	133	153	173
14	34	54	74	94	114	134	154	174
15	35	55	75	95	115	135	155	175
16	36	56	76	96	116	136	156	176
17	37	57	77	97	117	137	157	177
18	38	58	78	98	118	138	158	178
19	39	59	79	99	119	139	159	179
20	40	60	80	100	120	140	160	180

181	217	253	289	325	361	397	433	469
182	218	254	290	326	362	398	434	470
183	219	255	291	327	363	399	435	471
184	220	256	292	328	364	400	436	472
185	221	257	293	329	365	401	437	473
186	222	258	294	330	366	402	438	474
187	223	259	295	331	367	403	439	475
188	224	260	296	332	368	404	440	476
189	225	261	297	333	369	405	441	477
190	226	262	298	334	370	406	442	478
191	227	263	299	335	371	407	443	479
192	228	264	300	336	372	408	444	480
193	229	265	301	337	373	409	445	481
194	230	266	302	338	374	410	446	482
195	231	267	303	339	375	411	447	483
196	232	268	304	340	376	412	448	484
197	233	269	305	341	377	413	449	485
198	234	270	306	342	378	414	450	486
199	235	271	307	343	379	415	451	487
200	236	272	308	344	380	416	452	488
201	237	273	309	345	381	417	453	489
202	238	274	310	346	382	418	454	490
203	239	275	311	347	383	419	455	491
204	240	276	312	348	384	420	456	492
205	241	277	313	349	385	421	457	493
206	242	278	314	350	386	422	458	494
207	243	279	315	351	387	423	459	495
208	244	280	316	352	388	424	460	496
209	245	281	317	353	389	425	461	497
210	246	282	318	354	390	426	462	498
211	247	283	319	355	391	427	463	499
212	248	284	320	356	392	428	464	500
213	249	285	321	357	393	429	465	501*
214	250	286	322	358	394	430	466	
215	251	287	323	359	395	431	467	
216	252	288	324	360	396	432	468	

*Experimental.

First published 1948
This impression 1998

ISBN 0 7110 2585 1

All rights reserved. No part of this book may be reproduced in any form or by any means, electronic or mechanical, including photocopying, recording or by any information storage or retrieval system, without permission from the Publisher, in writing.

© Ian Allan Publishing Ltd 1948, 1998

Published by Ian Allan Publishing

an imprint of
Ian Allan Publishing Ltd, Terminal House, Station Approach, Shepperton, Surrey TW17 8AS.
Printed by Ian Allan Printing Ltd at its works at Riverdene, Molesey Road, Hersham, Surrey KT12 4RG.

Code: 9805/B2

This is a facsimile reprint of an original edition first published in 1948 and as such, with the exception of the advertisements below and on pages 86-88, all advertisements are no longer valid.

REMEMBERING BUSES THE WAY THEY USED TO BE

The bi-monthly magazine that recaptures the glories of older buses and trolleybuses with authoritative, entertaining and even provocative articles from the best writers, and first class photos in black-and-white and colour.

Classic Bus is available from good news-stands and newsagents

CLASSIC BUS

Subscriptions and other information:
CLASSIC BUS PUBLISHING LTD.
39 Lilyhill Terrace,
Edinburgh EH8 7DR

A NEW MAGAZINE FROM

Publishing

No self respecting bus preservationist can afford to be without a copy of *Preserved Bus*.

■ *Stunning photography*

■ *Wide ranging feature articles*

■ *Numerous regular features*

■ *News from the world of preserved buses and museums*

■ *Profiles of individual preserved buses*

■ *'Words of Wisdom' from experienced preservationists*

PRESERVED

BUS

Available from most good bookshops and newsagents or by subscription from:

**Ian Allan Subscriptions, Preserved Bus, 'Riverdene', Molesey Road, Hersham, Surrey KT12 4RG.
Tel 01932 266022. Fax: 01932 266033.**

(Subscription rates available on request).

Road transport titles from  Publishing

Bus Scene in Colour: London Buses
By Stephen Morris   ISBN: 071102555X   184mm x 240mmn   H/B
£13.99

Glory Days: RT — The History of a Classic London Bus
By Kevin McCormack   ISBN: 0711025819   184mm x 240mm   H/B   **£14.99**

The Heyday of the Routemaster
By Geoff Rixon   ISBN: 071102507X   184mm x 240mm   H/B
£12.99

The Heyday of the London Bus — 2
By Kevin McCormack   ISBN: 0711023441   184mm x 240mm   H/B   **£10.99**

The Heyday of the London Bus — 3
By Kevin McCormack   ISBN: 0711024863   184mm x 240mm   H/B   **£11.99**

London Country Buses in Colour
By Michael H. C. Baker   ISBN: 0711025576   184mm x 240mm   H/B   **£13.99**

How to order: These books are available from most good bookshops or mail order by calling **Ian Allan Mail Order Dept** on **01903 828800** (24 hour) quoting reference number **abcLT**, your credit card details and the ISBN(s) of the book(s). Alternatively, write to: **IAN ALLAN MAIL ORDER, Littlehampton Book Services, Dept abcLT, 10-14 Eldon Way, Lineside Estate, Littlehampton, West Sussex BN17 7HE.** Fax: 01903 828802 (Please add £2.50 post & packing charges UK, £3.60 overseas.)

For a copy of the Ian Allan Publishing book catalogue please write to:
The Marketing Department, Ian Allan Publishing Ltd, 'Riverdene', Molesey Road, Hersham, Surrey KT12 4RG.
Please include an A5 sae to the value of 50p. All titles available only while stocks last.

For all your transport requirements, visit the Ian Allan Bookshops in Birmingham, Manchester or London.

BIRMINGHAM	LONDON	MANCHESTER
Unit 84	45/46 Lower Marsh	Unit 5
47 Stephenson Street	Waterloo	Piccadilly Station
Birmingham B2 4DH	London SE1 7SG	Approach
Tel: 0121 643 2496	Tel: 0171 401 2100	Manchester M1 2GH
Fax: 0121 643 6855		Tel: 0161 237 9840
		Fax: 0161 237 9921

Each shop stocks a comprehensive range of books, magazines, videos, models, badges, postcards, calendars and much more!

For the full range of Ian Allan products plus books and videos from specialist publishers large and small - call into an Ian Allan Bookshop TODAY!

The Ian Allan Bookshops also offer a mail order service - please call for details.

To find out if an Ian Allan Bookshop is opening near you, please telephone: **0161 237 9840.**